TWO BY LUTHER

Two Classics by Martin Luther in One Affordable Volume

containing

CONCERNING CHRISTIAN LIBERTY

and

TREATISE ON GOOD WORKS

Martin Luther

LUMEN Christian Products®
Elizabethton, Tennessee

Martin Luther

German scholar, writer, teacher, theologian and religious reformer, Luther is one of the chief figures in European history. He initiated the Protestant Reformation; and in so doing changed the course of Western civilization.

CONTENTS

Letter to Pope Leo X 7

Concerning Christian Liberty 19

A Treatise on Good Works 57

Dedication 58

    The First and Second Commandments 61

    Thou Shalt Hallow the Day of Rest:
    The Third (Fourth) Commandment 93

    Thou Shalt Honor Thy Father and Thy Mother:
    The Fourth (Fifth) Commandment 120

    Thou Shalt Not Kill: The Fifth (Sixth) Commandment 140

    Thou Shalt Not Commit Adultery:
    The Sixth (Seventh) Commandment 143

    Thou Shalt Not Steal:
    The Seventh (Eighth) Commandment 146

    Thou Shalt Not Bear False Witness Against Thy Neighbor:
    The Eighth (Ninth) Commandment 150

    Thou Shalt Not Covet: The Ninth and Tenth
    Commandments(The Tenth Commandment) 154

APPENDIX 1: Martin Luther's 95 Theses 155

APPENDIX 2: Martin Luther's Address Before the
Diet of Worms 165

LETTER OF MARTIN LUTHER TO POPE LEO X.

Among those monstrous evils of this age with which I have now for three years been waging war, I am sometimes compelled to look to you and to call you to mind, most blessed father Leo. In truth, since you alone are everywhere considered as being the cause of my engaging in war, I cannot at any time fail to remember you; and although I have been compelled by the causeless raging of your impious flatterers against me to appeal from your seat to a future council--fearless of the futile decrees of your predecessors Pius and Julius, who in their foolish tyranny prohibited such an action--yet I have never been so alienated in feeling from your Blessedness as not to have sought with all my might, in diligent prayer and crying to God, all the best gifts for you and for your see. But those who have hitherto endeavored to terrify me with the majesty of your name and authority, I have begun quite to despise and triumph over. One thing I see remaining which I cannot despise, and this has been the reason of my writing anew to your Blessedness: namely, that I find that blame is cast on me, and that it is imputed to me as a great offence, that in my rashness I am judged to have spared not even your person.

Now, to confess the truth openly, I am conscious that, whenever I have had to mention your person, I have said nothing of you but what was honorable and good. If I had done otherwise, I could by no means have approved my own conduct, but should have supported with all my power the judgment of those men concerning me, nor would anything have pleased me better, than to recant such rashness and impiety. I have called you Daniel in Babylon; and every reader thoroughly knows with what distinguished zeal I defended your conspicuous innocence against Silvester, who tried to stain it. Indeed, the published opinion of so many great men and the repute of your blameless life are too widely famed and too much reverenced throughout the world to be assailable by any man, of however great name, or by any arts. I am not so foolish as to attack one whom everybody praises; nay, it has been and always will be my desire not to attack even those whom public repute disgraces. I am not delighted at the faults of any man, since I am very conscious myself of the great beam in my own eye, nor can I be the first to cast a stone at the adulteress.

I have indeed inveighed sharply against impious doctrines, and I have not been slack to censure my adversaries on account, not of their bad morals, but of their impiety. And for this I am so far from being sorry that I have brought my mind to despise the judgments of men and to persevere in this vehement zeal, according to the example of Christ, who, in His zeal, calls His adversaries a generation of vipers, blind, hypocrites, and children of the devil. Paul, too, charges the sorcerer with being a child of the devil, full of all subtlety and all malice; and defames certain persons as evil workers, dogs, and deceivers. In the opinion of those delicate-eared persons, nothing could be more bitter or intemperate than Paul's language. What can be more bitter than the words of the prophets? The ears of our generation have been made so delicate by the senseless multitude of flatterers that, as soon as we perceive that anything of ours is not approved of, we cry out that we are being bitterly assailed; and when we can repel the truth by no other pretence, we escape by attributing bitterness, impatience, intemperance, to our adversaries. What would be the use of salt if it were not pungent, or of the edge of the sword if it did not slay? Accursed is the man who does the work of the Lord deceitfully.

Wherefore, most excellent Leo, I beseech you to accept my vindication, made in this letter, and to persuade yourself that I have never thought any evil concerning your person; further, that I am one who desires that eternal blessing may fall to your lot, and that I have no dispute with any man concerning morals, but only concerning the word of truth. In all other things I will yield to anyone, but I neither can nor will forsake and deny the word. He who thinks otherwise of me, or has taken in my words in another sense, does not think rightly, and has not taken in the truth.

Your see, however, which is called the Court of Rome, and which neither you nor any man can deny to be more corrupt than any Babylon or Sodom, and quite, as I believe, of a lost, desperate, and hopeless impiety, this I have verily abominated, and have felt indignant that the people of Christ should be cheated under your name and the pretext of the Church of Rome; and so I have resisted, and will resist, as long as the spirit of faith shall live in me. Not that I am striving after impossibilities, or hoping that by my labors alone, against the furious opposition of so many flatterers, any good can be done in that most disordered Babylon; but that I feel myself a debtor to my brethren, and am bound to take thought for them, that fewer of them may be ruined, or that their ruin may be less complete, by the plagues of Rome. For many years now, nothing else has overflowed from Rome into the world--as you are not ignorant--than the laying waste of goods, of bodies, and of souls, and the worst examples of all the worst things. These things are clearer than the light to all men; and the Church of Rome, formerly the most holy of all Churches, has become the most lawless den of thieves, the most shameless of all brothels, the very kingdom of sin, death, and hell; so that not even antichrist, if he were to come, could devise any addition to its wickedness.

Meanwhile you, Leo, are sitting like a lamb in the midst of wolves, like Daniel in the midst of lions, and, with Ezekiel, you dwell among scorpions. What opposition can you alone make to these monstrous evils? Take to yourself three or four of the most learned and best of the cardinals. What are these among so many? You would all perish by poison before you could undertake to decide on a remedy. It is all over with the Court of Rome; the wrath of God has come upon her to the uttermost. She hates councils; she dreads to be reformed; she cannot restrain the madness of her impiety; she fills up the sentence passed on her mother, of whom it is said, "We would have healed Babylon, but she is not healed; let us forsake her." It had been your duty and that of your cardinals to apply a remedy to these evils, but this gout laughs at the physician's hand, and the chariot does not obey the reins. Under the influence of these feelings, I have always grieved that you, most excellent Leo, who were worthy of a better age, have been made pontiff in this. For the Roman Court is not worthy of you and those like you, but of Satan himself, who in truth is more the ruler in that Babylon than you are.

Oh, would that, having laid aside that glory which your most abandoned enemies declare to be yours, you were living rather in the office of a private priest or on your paternal inheritance! In that glory none are worthy to glory, except the race of Iscariot, the children of perdition. For what happens in your court, Leo, except that, the more wicked and execrable any man is, the more prosperously he can use your name and authority for the ruin of the property and souls of men, for the multiplication of crimes, for the oppression of faith and truth and of the whole Church of God? Oh, Leo! in reality most unfortunate, and sitting on a most perilous throne, I tell you the truth, because I wish you well; for if Bernard felt compassion for his Anastasius at a time when the Roman see, though even then most corrupt, was as yet ruling with better hope than now, why should not we lament, to whom so much further corruption and ruin has been added in three hundred years?

Is it not true that there is nothing under the vast heavens more corrupt, more pestilential, more hateful, than the Court of Rome? She incomparably surpasses the impiety of the Turks, so that in very truth she, who was formerly the gate of heaven, is now a sort of open mouth of hell, and such a mouth as, under the urgent wrath of God, cannot be blocked up; one course alone being left to us wretched men: to call back and save some few, if we can, from that Roman gulf.

Behold, Leo, my father, with what purpose and on what principle it is that I have stormed against that seat of pestilence. I am so far from having felt any rage against your person that I even hoped to gain favor with you and to aid you in your welfare by striking actively and vigorously at that your prison, nay, your hell. For whatever the efforts of all minds can contrive against the confusion of that impious Court will be advantageous to you and to your welfare, and to many others with you. Those who do harm to her are doing your office; those who in every way abhor her are glorifying Christ; in short, those are Christians who are not Romans.

But, to say yet more, even this never entered my heart: to inveigh against the Court of Rome or to dispute at all about her. For, seeing all remedies for her health to be desperate, I looked on her with contempt, and, giving her a bill of divorcement, said to her, "He that is unjust, let him be unjust still; and he that is filthy, let him be filthy still," giving myself up to the peaceful and quiet study of sacred literature, that by this I might be of use to the brethren living about me.

While I was making some advance in these studies, Satan opened his eyes and goaded on his servant John Eccius, that notorious adversary of Christ, by the unchecked lust for fame, to drag me unexpectedly into the arena, trying to catch me in one little word concerning the primacy of the Church of Rome, which had fallen from me in passing. That boastful Thraso, foaming and gnashing his teeth, proclaimed that he would dare all things for the glory of God and for the honor of the holy apostolic seat; and, being puffed up respecting your power, which he was about to misuse, he looked forward with all certainty to victory; seeking to promote, not so much the primacy of Peter, as his own pre-eminence among the theologians of this age; for he thought it would contribute in no slight degree to this, if he were to lead Luther in triumph. The result having proved unfortunate for the sophist, an incredible rage torments him; for he feels that whatever discredit to Rome has arisen through me has been caused by the fault of himself alone.

Suffer me, I pray you, most excellent Leo, both to plead my own cause, and to accuse your true enemies. I believe it is known to you in what way Cardinal Cajetan, your imprudent and unfortunate, nay unfaithful, legate, acted towards me. When, on account of my reverence for your name, I had placed myself and all that was mine in his hands, he did not so act as to establish peace, which he could easily have established by one little word, since I at that time promised to be silent and to make an end of my case, if he would command my adversaries to do the same. But that man of pride, not content with this agreement, began to justify my adversaries, to give them free license, and to order me to recant, a thing which was certainly not in his commission. Thus indeed, when the case was in the best position, it came through his vexatious tyranny into a much worse one. Therefore whatever has followed upon this is the fault not of Luther, but entirely of Cajetan, since he did not suffer me to be silent and remain quiet, which at that time I was entreating for with all my might. What more was it my duty to do?

Next came Charles Miltitz, also a nuncio from your Blessedness. He, though he went up and down with much and varied exertion, and omitted nothing which could tend to restore the position of the cause thrown into confusion by the rashness and pride of Cajetan, had difficulty, even with the help of that very illustrious prince the Elector Frederick, in at last bringing about more than one familiar conference with me. In these I again yielded to your great name, and was prepared to keep silence, and to accept as my judge either the Archbishop of Treves, or the Bishop of Naumburg; and thus it was done and concluded. While this was being done with good hope of success, lo! that other and greater enemy of yours, Eccius, rushed in with his Leipsic disputation, which he had undertaken against Carlstadt, and, having taken up a new question concerning the primacy of the Pope, turned his arms unexpectedly against me, and completely overthrew the plan for peace. Meanwhile Charles Miltitz was waiting, disputations were held, judges were being chosen, but no decision was arrived at. And no wonder! for by the falsehoods, pretences, and arts of Eccius the whole business was brought into such thorough disorder, confusion, and festering soreness, that, whichever way the sentence might lean, a greater conflagration was sure to arise; for he was seeking, not after truth, but after his own credit. In this case too I omitted nothing which it was right that I should do.

I confess that on this occasion no small part of the corruptions of Rome came to light; but, if there was any offence in this, it was the fault of Eccius, who, in taking on him a burden beyond his strength,

13

and in furiously aiming at credit for himself, unveiled to the whole world the disgrace of Rome.

Here is that enemy of yours, Leo, or rather of your Court; by his example alone we may learn that an enemy is not more baneful than a flatterer. For what did he bring about by his flattery, except evils which no king could have brought about? At this day the name of the Court of Rome stinks in the nostrils of the world, the papal authority is growing weak, and its notorious ignorance is evil spoken of. We should hear none of these things, if Eccius had not disturbed the plans of Miltitz and myself for peace. He feels this clearly enough himself in the indignation he shows, too late and in vain, against the publication of my books. He ought to have reflected on this at the time when he was all mad for renown, and was seeking in your cause nothing but his own objects, and that with the greatest peril to you. The foolish man hoped that, from fear of your name, I should yield and keep silence; for I do not think he presumed on his talents and learning. Now, when he sees that I am very confident and speak aloud, he repents too late of his rashness, and sees--if indeed he does see it--that there is One in heaven who resists the proud, and humbles the presumptuous.

Since then we were bringing about by this disputation nothing but the greater confusion of the cause of Rome, Charles Miltitz for the third time addressed the Fathers of the Order, assembled in chapter, and sought their advice for the settlement of the case, as being now in a most troubled and perilous state. Since, by the favor of God, there was no hope of proceeding against me by force, some of the more noted of their number were sent to me, and begged me at least to show respect to your person and to vindicate in a humble letter both your innocence and my own. They said that the affair was not as yet in a position of extreme hopelessness, if Leo X., in his inborn kindliness, would put his hand to it. On this I, who have always offered and wished for peace, in order that I might devote myself to calmer and more useful pursuits, and who for this very purpose have acted with so much spirit and vehemence, in order to put down by the strength and impetuosity of my words, as well as of my feelings, men whom I saw to be very far from equal to myself--I, I say, not only gladly yielded, but even accepted it with joy and gratitude, as the greatest kindness and benefit, if you should think it right to satisfy my hopes.

Thus I come, most blessed Father, and in all abasement beseech you to put to your hand, if it is possible, and impose a curb to those flatterers who are enemies of peace, while they pretend peace. But there is no reason, most blessed Father, why anyone should assume that I am to utter a recantation, unless he prefers to involve the case in still greater confusion. Moreover, I cannot bear with laws for the interpretation of the word of God, since the word of God, which teaches liberty in all other things, ought not to be bound. Saving these two things, there is nothing which I am not able, and most heartily willing, to do or to suffer. I hate contention; I will challenge no one; in return I wish not to be challenged; but, being challenged, I will not be dumb in the cause of Christ my Master. For your Blessedness will be able by one short and easy word to call these controversies before you and suppress them, and to impose silence and peace on both sides--a word which I have ever longed to hear.

Therefore, Leo, my Father, beware of listening to those sirens who make you out to be not simply a man, but partly a god, so that you can command and require whatever you will. It will not happen so, nor will you prevail. You are the servant of servants, and more than any other man, in a most pitiable and perilous position. Let not those men deceive you who pretend that you are lord of the world; who will not allow anyone to be a Christian without your authority; who babble of your having power over heaven, hell, and purgatory. These men are your enemies and are seeking your soul to destroy it, as Isaiah says, "My people, they that call thee blessed are themselves deceiving thee." They are in error who raise you above councils and the universal Church; they are in error who attribute to you alone the right of interpreting Scripture. All these men are seeking to set up their own impieties in the Church under your name, and alas! Satan has gained much through them in the time of your predecessors.

In brief, trust not in any who exalt you, but in those who humiliate you. For this is the judgment of God: "He hath cast down the mighty from their seat, and hath exalted the humble." See how unlike Christ was to His successors, though all will have it that they are His vicars. I fear that in truth very many of them have been in too serious a sense His vicars, for a vicar represents a prince who is absent. Now if a pontiff rules while Christ is absent and does not dwell in his heart, what else is he but a vicar of Christ? And then what is that Church but a multitude without Christ? What indeed is such a vicar but antichrist and an idol? How much more rightly did the Apostles speak, who call themselves servants of a present Christ, not the vicars of an absent one!

Perhaps I am shamelessly bold in seeming to teach so great a head, by whom all men ought to be taught, and from whom, as those plagues of yours boast, the thrones of judges receive their sentence; but I imitate St. Bernard in his book concerning Considerations addressed to Eugenius, a book which ought to be known by heart by every pontiff. I do this, not from any desire to teach, but as a duty, from that simple and faithful solicitude which teaches us to be anxious for all that is safe for our neighbors, and does not allow considerations of worthiness or unworthiness to be entertained, being intent only on the dangers or advantage of others. For since I know that your Blessedness is driven and tossed by the waves at Rome, so that the depths of the sea press on you with infinite perils, and that you are laboring under such a condition of misery that you need even the least help from any the least brother, I do not seem to myself to be acting unsuitably if I forget your majesty till I shall have fulfilled the office of charity. I will not flatter in so serious and perilous a matter; and if in this you do not see that I am your friend and most thoroughly your subject, there is One to see and judge.

In fine, that I may not approach you empty-handed, blessed Father, I bring with me this little treatise, published under your name, as a good omen of the establishment of peace and of good hope. By this you may perceive in what pursuits I should prefer and be able to occupy myself to more profit, if I were allowed, or had been hitherto allowed, by your impious flatterers. It is a small matter, if you look to its exterior, but, unless I mistake, it is a summary of the Christian life put together in small compass, if you apprehend its meaning. I, in my poverty, have no other present to make you, nor do you need anything else than to be enriched by a spiritual gift. I commend myself to your Paternity and Blessedness, whom may the Lord Jesus preserve forever. Amen.

Wittenberg, 6th September, 1520.

CONCERNING
CHRISTIAN LIBERTY

Christian faith has appeared to many an easy thing; nay, not a few even reckon it among the social virtues, as it were; and this they do because they have not made proof of it experimentally, and have never tasted of what efficacy it is. For it is not possible for any man to write well about it, or to understand well what is rightly written, who has not at some time tasted of its spirit, under the pressure of tribulation; while he who has tasted of it, even to a very small extent, can never write, speak, think, or hear about it sufficiently. For it is a living fountain, springing up into eternal life, as Christ calls it in John chapter 4.

Now, though I cannot boast of my abundance, and though I know how poorly I am furnished, yet I hope that, after having been vexed by various temptations, I have attained some little drop of faith, and that I can speak of this matter, if not with more elegance, certainly with more solidity, than those literal and too subtle disputants who have hitherto discoursed upon it without understanding their own words. That I may open then an easier way for the ignorant--for these alone I am trying to serve--I first lay down these two propositions, concerning spiritual liberty and servitude:

1. A Christian man is the most free lord of all,
   and subject to none;

2. A Christian man is the most dutiful servant of all,
   and subject to everyone.

Although these statements appear contradictory, yet, when they are found to agree together, they will make excellently for my purpose. They are both the statements of Paul himself, who says, "Though I be free from all men, yet have I made myself servant unto all" (1 Corinthians 9:19), and "Owe no man anything, but to love one another" (Romans 13:8). Now love is by its own nature dutiful and obedient to the beloved object. Thus even Christ, though Lord of all things, was yet made of a woman; made under the law; at once free and a servant; at once in the form of God and in the form of a servant.

Let us examine the subject on a deeper and less simple principle. Man is composed of a twofold nature, a spiritual and a bodily. As regards the spiritual nature, which they name the soul, he is called the spiritual, inward, new man; as regards the bodily nature, which they name the flesh, he is called the fleshly, outward, old man. The Apostle speaks of this: "Though our outward man perish, yet the inward man is renewed day by day" (2 Corinthians 4:16). The result of this diversity is that in the Scriptures opposing statements are made concerning the same man, the fact being that in the same man these two men are opposed to one another; the flesh lusting against the spirit, and the spirit against the flesh (Galatians 5:17).

We first approach the subject of the inward man, that we may see by what means a man becomes justified, free, and a true Christian; that is, a spiritual, new, and inward man. It is certain that absolutely none among outward things, under whatever name they may be reckoned, has any influence in producing Christian righteousness or liberty, nor, on the other hand, unrighteousness or slavery. This can be shown by an easy argument.

What can it profit the soul that the body should be in good condition, free, and full of life; that it should eat, drink, and act according to its pleasure; when even the most impious slaves of every kind of vice are prosperous in these matters? Again, what harm can ill-health, bondage, hunger, thirst, or any other outward evil, do to the soul, when even the most pious of men and the freest in the purity of their conscience, are harassed by these things? Neither of these states of things has to do with the liberty or the slavery of the soul.

And so it will profit nothing that the body should be adorned with sacred vestments, or dwell in holy places, or be occupied in sacred offices, or pray, fast, and abstain from certain meats, or do whatever works can be done through the body and in the body. Something widely different will be necessary for the justification and liberty of the soul, since the things I have spoken of can be done by any impious person, and only hypocrites are produced by devotion to these things.

21

On the other hand, it will not at all injure the soul that the body should be clothed in profane raiment, should dwell in profane places, should eat and drink in the ordinary fashion, should not pray aloud, and should leave undone all the things above mentioned, which may be done by hypocrites.

And, to cast everything aside, even speculation, meditations, and whatever things can be performed by the exertions of the soul itself, are of no profit. One thing, and one alone, is necessary for life, justification, and Christian liberty; and that is the most holy word of God, the Gospel of Christ, as He says, "I am the resurrection and the life; he that believeth in Me shall not die eternally" (John 11:25), and also, "If the Son shall make you free, ye shall be free indeed" (John 8:36), and, "Man shall not live by bread alone, but by every word that proceedeth out of the mouth of God" (Matthew 4:4).

Let us therefore hold it for certain and firmly established that the soul can do without everything except the word of God, without which none at all of its wants are provided for. But, having the word, it is rich and wants for nothing, since that is the word of life, of truth, of light, of peace, of justification, of salvation, of joy, of liberty, of wisdom, of virtue, of grace, of glory, and of every good thing. It is on this account that the prophet in a whole Psalm (Psalm 119.), and in many other places, sighs for and calls upon the word of God with so many groanings and words.

Again, there is no more cruel stroke of the wrath of God than when He sends a famine of hearing His words (Amos 8:11), just as there is no greater favor from Him than the sending forth of His word, as it is said, "He sent His word and healed them, and delivered them from their destructions" (Psalm 107:20). Christ was sent for no other office than that of the word; and the order of Apostles, that of bishops, and that of the whole body of the clergy, have been called and instituted for no object but the ministry of the word.

But you will ask what is this word, and by what means is it to be used, since there are so many words of God? I answer, The Apostle

Paul (Romans 1) explains what it is, namely the Gospel of God, concerning His Son, incarnate, suffering, risen, and glorified, through the Spirit, the Sanctifier. To preach Christ is to feed the soul, to justify it, to set it free, and to save it, if it believes the preaching. For faith alone and the efficacious use of the word of God, bring salvation. "If thou shalt confess with thy mouth the Lord Jesus, and shalt believe in thine heart that God hath raised Him from the dead, thou shalt be saved" (Romans 10:9); and again, "Christ is the end of the law for righteousness to everyone that believeth" (Romans 10:4), and "The just shall live by faith" (Romans 1:7). For the word of God cannot be received and honored by any works, but by faith alone. Hence it is clear that as the soul needs the word alone for life and justification, so it is justified by faith alone, and not by any works. For if it could be justified by any other means, it would have no need of the word, nor consequently of faith.

But this faith cannot consist at all with works; that is, if you imagine that you can be justified by those works, whatever they are, along with it. For this would be to halt between two opinions, to worship Baal, and to kiss the hand to him, which is a very great iniquity, as Job says. Therefore, when you begin to believe, you learn at the same time that all that is in you is utterly guilty, sinful, and damnable, according to that saying, "All have sinned, and come short of the glory of God" (Romans 3:23), and also: "There is none righteous, no, not one; they are all gone out of the way; they are together become unprofitable: there is none that doeth good, no, not one" (Romans 3:10-12). When you have learnt this, you will know that Christ is necessary for you, since He has suffered and risen again for you, that, believing on Him, you might by this faith become another man, all your sins being remitted, and you being justified by the merits of another, namely of Christ alone.

Since then this faith can reign only in the inward man, as it is said, "With the heart man believeth unto righteousness" (Romans 10:10); and since it alone justifies, it is evident that by no outward work or labor can the inward man be at all justified, made free, and saved;

and that no works whatever have any relation to him. And so, on the other hand, it is solely by impiety and incredulity of heart that he becomes guilty and a slave of sin, deserving condemnation, not by any outward sin or work. Therefore the first care of every Christian ought to be to lay aside all reliance on works, and strengthen his faith alone more and more, and by it grow in the knowledge, not of works, but of Christ Jesus, who has suffered and risen again for him, as Peter teaches (1 Peter 5) when he makes no other work to be a Christian one. Thus Christ, when the Jews asked Him what they should do that they might work the works of God, rejected the multitude of works, with which He saw that they were puffed up, and commanded them one thing only, saying, "This is the work of God: that ye believe on Him whom He hath sent, for Him hath God the Father sealed" (John 6:27, 29).

Hence a right faith in Christ is an incomparable treasure, carrying with it universal salvation and preserving from all evil, as it is said, "He that believeth and is baptized shall be saved; but he that believeth not shall be damned" (Mark 16:16). Isaiah, looking to this treasure, predicted, "The consumption decreed shall overflow with righteousness. For the Lord God of hosts shall make a consumption, even determined (*verbum abbreviatum et consummans*), in the midst of the land" (Isaiah 10:22, 23). As if he said, "Faith, which is the brief and complete fulfilling of the law, will fill those who believe with such righteousness that they will need nothing else for justification." Thus, too, Paul says, "For with the heart man believeth unto righteousness" (Romans 10:10).

But you ask how it can be the fact that faith alone justifies, and affords without works so great a treasure of good things, when so many works, ceremonies, and laws are prescribed to us in the Scriptures? I answer; before all things bear in mind what I have said: that faith alone without works justifies, sets free, and saves, as I shall show more clearly below.

*****

Meanwhile it is to be noted that the whole Scripture of God is divided into two parts: precepts and promises. The precepts certainly teach us what is good, but what they teach is not forthwith done. For they show us what we ought to do, but do not give us the power to do it. They were ordained, however, for the purpose of showing man to himself, that through them he may learn his own impotence for good and may despair of his own strength. For this reason they are called the Old Testament, and are so.

For example, "Thou shalt not covet," is a precept by which we are all convicted of sin, since no man can help coveting, whatever efforts to the contrary he may make. In order therefore that he may fulfill the precept, and not covet, he is constrained to despair of himself and to seek elsewhere and through another the help which he cannot find in himself; as it is said, "O Israel, thou hast destroyed thyself; but in Me is thine help" (Hosea 13:9). Now what is done by this one precept is done by all; for all are equally impossible of fulfillment by us.

Now when a man has through the precepts been taught his own impotence, and become anxious by what means he may satisfy the law--for the law must be satisfied, so that no jot or tittle of it may pass away, otherwise he must be hopelessly condemned--then, being truly humbled and brought to nothing in his own eyes, he finds in himself no resource for justification and salvation.

Then comes in that other part of Scripture, the promises of God, which declare the glory of God, and say, "If you wish to fulfill the law, and, as the law requires, not to covet, lo! believe in Christ, in whom are promised to you grace, justification, peace, and liberty." All these things you shall have, if you believe, and shall be without them if you do not believe. For what is impossible for you by all the works of the law, which are many and yet useless, you shall fulfill in an easy and summary way through faith, because God the Father has made everything to depend on faith, so that whosoever has it has all things, and he who has it not has nothing. "For God hath concluded them all in unbelief, that He might have mercy upon all" (Romans 11:32). Thus the promises of God give that which the precepts exact, and fulfill what the law commands; so that all is of God alone, both the precepts and their fulfillment. He alone commands; He alone also fulfils. Hence the promises of God belong to the New Testament; nay, are the New Testament.

Now, since these promises of God are words of holiness, truth, righteousness, liberty, and peace, and are full of universal goodness, the soul, which cleaves to them with a firm faith, is so united to them, nay, thoroughly absorbed by them, that it not only partakes in, but is penetrated and saturated by, all their virtues. For if the touch of Christ was healing, how much more does that most tender spiritual touch, nay, absorption of the word, communicate to the soul all that belongs to the word! In this way therefore the soul, through faith alone, without works, is from the word of God justified, sanctified, endued with truth, peace, and liberty, and filled full with every good thing, and is truly made the child of God, as it is said, "To them gave He power to become the sons of God, even to them that believe on His name" (John 1:12).

From all this it is easy to understand why faith has such great power, and why no good works, nor even all good works put together, can compare with it, since no work can cleave to the word of God or be in the soul. Faith alone and the word reign in it; and such as is the word, such is the soul made by it, just as iron exposed to fire glows like fire, on account of its union with the fire. It is clear then that to a Christian man his faith suffices for everything, and that he has no need of works for justification. But if he has no need of works, neither has he need of the law; and if he has no need of the law, he is certainly free from the law, and the saying is true, "The law is not made for a righteous man" (1 Timothy 1:9). This is that Christian liberty, our faith, the effect of which is, not that we should be careless or lead a bad life, but that no one should need the law or works for justification and salvation.

Let us consider this as the first virtue of faith; and let us look also to the second. This also is an office of faith: that it honors with the utmost veneration and the highest reputation Him in whom it believes, inasmuch as it holds Him to be truthful and worthy of belief. For there is no honor like that reputation of truth and righteousness with which we honor Him in whom we believe. What higher credit can we attribute to any one than truth and righteousness, and absolute goodness? On the other hand, it is the greatest insult to brand any one with the reputation of falsehood and unrighteousness, or to suspect him of these, as we do when we disbelieve him.

Thus the soul, in firmly believing the promises of God, holds Him to be true and righteous; and it can attribute to God no higher glory than the credit of being so. The highest worship of God is to ascribe to Him truth, righteousness, and whatever qualities we must ascribe to one in whom we believe. In doing this the soul shows itself prepared to do His whole will; in doing this it hallows His name, and gives itself up to be dealt with as it may please God. For it cleaves to His promises, and never doubts that He is true, just, and wise, and will do, dispose, and provide for all things in the best way. Is not such a soul, in this its faith, most obedient to God in all things? What commandment does there remain which has not been amply fulfilled by such an obedience? What fulfillment can be more full than universal obedience? Now this is not accomplished by works, but by faith alone.

On the other hand, what greater rebellion, impiety, or insult to God can there be, than not to believe His promises? What else is this, than either to make God a liar, or to doubt His truth--that is, to attribute truth to ourselves, but to God falsehood and levity? In doing this, is not a man denying God and setting himself up as an idol in his own heart? What then can works, done in such a state of impiety, profit us, were they even angelic or apostolic works? Rightly hath God shut up all, not in wrath nor in lust, but in unbelief, in order that those who pretend that they are fulfilling the law by works of purity and benevolence (which are social and human virtues) may not presume that they will therefore be saved, but, being included in the sin of unbelief, may either seek mercy, or be justly condemned.

But when God sees that truth is ascribed to Him, and that in the faith of our hearts He is honored with all the honor of which He is worthy, then in return He honors us on account of that faith, attributing to us truth and righteousness. For faith does truth and righteousness in rendering to God what is His; and therefore in return God gives glory to our righteousness. It is true and righteous that God is true and righteous; and to confess this and ascribe these attributes to Him, this it is to be true and righteous. Thus He says, "Them that honor Me I will honor, and they that despise Me shall be lightly esteemed" (1 Samuel 2:30). And so Paul says that Abraham's faith was imputed to him for righteousness, because by it he gave glory to God; and that to us also, for the same reason, it shall be imputed for righteousness, if we believe (Romans 4).

The third incomparable grace of faith is this: that it unites the soul to Christ, as the wife to the husband, by which mystery, as the Apostle teaches, Christ and the soul are made one flesh. Now if they are one flesh, and if a true marriage--nay, by far the most perfect of all marriages--is accomplished between them (for human marriages are but feeble types of this one great marriage), then it follows that all they have becomes theirs in common, as well good things as evil things; so that whatsoever Christ possesses, that the believing soul may take to itself and boast of as its own, and whatever belongs to the soul, that Christ claims as His.

If we compare these possessions, we shall see how inestimable is the gain. Christ is full of grace, life, and salvation; the soul is full of sin, death, and condemnation. Let faith step in, and then sin, death, and hell will belong to Christ, and grace, life, and salvation to the soul. For, if He is a Husband, He must needs take to Himself that which is His wife's, and at the same time, impart to His wife that which is His. For, in giving her His own body and Himself, how can He but give her all that is His? And, in taking to Himself the body of His wife, how can He but take to Himself all that is hers?

In this is displayed the delightful sight, not only of communion, but of a prosperous warfare, of victory, salvation, and redemption. For, since Christ is God and man, and is such a Person as neither has sinned, nor dies, nor is condemned, nay, cannot sin, die, or be condemned, and since His righteousness, life, and salvation are invincible, eternal, and almighty,--when I say, such a Person, by the wedding-ring of faith, takes a share in the sins, death, and hell of His wife, nay, makes them His own, and deals with them no otherwise than as if they were His, and as if He Himself had sinned; and when He suffers, dies, and descends to hell, that He may overcome all things, and since sin, death, and hell cannot swallow Him up, they must needs be swallowed up by Him in stupendous conflict. For His righteousness rises above the sins of all men; His life is more powerful than all death; His salvation is more unconquerable than all hell.

Thus the believing soul, by the pledge of its faith in Christ, becomes free from all sin, fearless of death, safe from hell, and endowed with the eternal righteousness, life, and salvation of its Husband Christ. Thus He presents to Himself a glorious bride, without spot or wrinkle, cleansing her with the washing of water by the word; that is, by faith in the word of life, righteousness, and salvation. Thus He betrothes her unto Himself "in faithfulness, in righteousness, and in judgment, and in loving-kindness, and in mercies" (Hosea 2:19, 20).

Who then can value highly enough these royal nuptials? Who can comprehend the riches of the glory of this grace? Christ, that rich and pious Husband, takes as a wife a needy and impious harlot, redeeming her from all her evils and supplying her with all His good things. It is impossible now that her sins should destroy her, since they have been laid upon Christ and swallowed up in Him, and since she has in her Husband Christ a righteousness which she may claim as her own, and which she can set up with confidence against all her sins, against death and hell, saying, "If I have sinned, my Christ, in whom I believe, has not sinned; all mine is His, and all His is mine," as it is written, "My beloved is mine, and I am His" (Song of Solomon 2:16). This is what Paul says: "Thanks be to God, which giveth us the victory through our Lord Jesus Christ," victory over sin and death, as he says, "The sting of death is sin, and the strength of sin is the law" (1 Corinthians 15:56, 57).

From all this you will again understand why so much importance is attributed to faith, so that it alone can fulfill the law and justify without any works. For you see that the First Commandment, which says, "Thou shalt worship one God only," is fulfilled by faith alone. If you were nothing but good works from the soles of your feet to the crown of your head, you would not be worshipping God, nor fulfilling the First Commandment, since it is impossible to worship God without ascribing to Him the glory of truth and of universal goodness, as it ought in truth to be ascribed. Now this is not done by works, but only by faith of heart. It is not by working, but by believing, that we glorify God, and confess Him to be true. On this ground faith alone is the righteousness of a Christian man, and the fulfilling of all the commandments. For to him who fulfils the first the task of fulfilling all the rest is easy.

*****

Works, since they are irrational things, cannot glorify God, although they may be done to the glory of God, if faith be present. But at present we are inquiring, not into the quality of the works done, but into him who does them, who glorifies God, and brings forth good works. This is faith of heart, the head and the substance of all our righteousness. Hence that is a blind and perilous doctrine which teaches that the commandments are fulfilled by works. The commandments must have been fulfilled previous to any good works, and good works follow their fulfillment, as we shall see.

But, that we may have a wider view of that grace which our inner man has in Christ, we must know that in the Old Testament God sanctified to Himself every first-born male. The birthright was of great value, giving a superiority over the rest by the double honor of priesthood and kingship. For the first-born brother was priest and lord of all the rest.

Under this figure was foreshown Christ, the true and only First-born of God the Father and of the Virgin Mary, and a true King and Priest, not in a fleshly and earthly sense. For His kingdom is not of this world; it is in heavenly and spiritual things that He reigns and acts as Priest; and these are righteousness, truth, wisdom, peace, salvation, etc. Not but that all things, even those of earth and hell, are subject to Him--for otherwise how could He defend and save us from them?--but it is not in these, nor by these, that His kingdom stands.

So, too, His priesthood does not consist in the outward display of vestments and gestures, as did the human priesthood of Aaron and our ecclesiastical priesthood at this day, but in spiritual things, wherein, in His invisible office, He intercedes for us with God in heaven, and there offers Himself, and performs all the duties of a priest, as Paul describes Him to the Hebrews under the figure of Melchizedek. Nor does He only pray and intercede for us; He also teaches us inwardly in the spirit with the living teachings of His Spirit. Now these are the two special offices of a priest, as is figured to us in the case of fleshly priests by visible prayers and sermons.

As Christ by His birthright has obtained these two dignities, so He imparts and communicates them to every believer in Him, under that law of matrimony of which we have spoken above, by which all that is the husband's is also the wife's. Hence all we who believe on Christ are kings and priests in Christ, as it is said, "Ye are a chosen generation, a royal priesthood, a holy nation, a peculiar people, that ye should show forth the praises of Him who hath called you out of darkness into His marvelous light" (1 Peter 2:9).

These two things stand thus. First, as regards kingship, every Christian is by faith so exalted above all things that, in spiritual power, he is completely lord of all things, so that nothing whatever can do him any hurt; yea, all things are subject to him, and are compelled to be subservient to his salvation. Thus Paul says, "All things work together for good to them who are the called" (Romans 8:28), and also, "Whether life, or death, or things present, or things to come, all are yours; and ye are Christ's" (1 Corinthians 3:22, 23).

Not that in the sense of corporeal power any one among Christians has been appointed to possess and rule all things, according to the mad and senseless idea of certain ecclesiastics. That is the office of kings, princes, and men upon earth. In the experience of life we see that we are subjected to all things, and suffer many things, even death. Yea, the more of a Christian any man is, to so many the more evils, sufferings, and deaths is he subject, as we see in the first place in Christ the First-born, and in all His holy brethren.

This is a spiritual power, which rules in the midst of enemies, and is powerful in the midst of distresses. And this is nothing else than that strength is made perfect in my weakness, and that I can turn all things to the profit of my salvation; so that even the cross and death are compelled to serve me and to work together for my salvation. This is a lofty and eminent dignity, a true and almighty dominion, a spiritual empire, in which there is nothing so good, nothing so bad, as not to work together for my good, if only I believe. And yet there is nothing of which I have need--for faith alone suffices for my salvation--unless that in it faith may exercise the power and empire of its liberty. This is the inestimable power and liberty of Christians.

Nor are we only kings and the freest of all men, but also priests forever, a dignity far higher than kingship, because by that priesthood we are worthy to appear before God, to pray for others, and to teach one another mutually the things which are of God. For these are the duties of priests, and they cannot possibly be permitted to any unbeliever. Christ has obtained for us this favor, if we believe in Him:

that just as we are His brethren and co-heirs and fellow-kings with Him, so we should be also fellow-priests with Him, and venture with confidence, through the spirit of faith, to come into the presence of God, and cry, "Abba, Father!" and to pray for one another, and to do all things which we see done and figured in the visible and corporeal office of priesthood. But to an unbelieving person nothing renders service or work for good. He himself is in servitude to all things, and all things turn out for evil to him, because he uses all things in an impious way for his own advantage, and not for the glory of God. And thus he is not a priest, but a profane person, whose prayers are turned into sin, nor does he ever appear in the presence of God, because God does not hear sinners.

Who then can comprehend the loftiness of that Christian dignity which, by its royal power, rules over all things, even over death, life, and sin, and, by its priestly glory, is all-powerful with God, since God does what He Himself seeks and wishes, as it is written, "He will fulfill the desire of them that fear Him; He also will hear their cry, and will save them"? (Psalm 145:19). This glory certainly cannot be attained by any works, but by faith only.

From these considerations any one may clearly see how a Christian man is free from all things; so that he needs no works in order to be justified and saved, but receives these gifts in abundance from faith alone. Nay, were he so foolish as to pretend to be justified, set free, saved, and made a Christian, by means of any good work, he would immediately lose faith, with all its benefits. Such folly is prettily represented in the fable where a dog, running along in the water and carrying in his mouth a real piece of meat, is deceived by the reflection of the meat in the water, and, in trying with open mouth to seize it, loses the meat and its image at the same time.

Here you will ask, "If all who are in the Church are priests, by what character are those whom we now call priests to be distinguished from the laity?" I reply, By the use of these words, "priest," "clergy," "spiritual person," "ecclesiastic," an injustice has been done, since they have been transferred from the remaining body of Christians to those few who are now, by hurtful custom, called ecclesiastics. For Holy Scripture makes no distinction between them, except that those who are now boastfully called popes, bishops, and lords, it calls ministers, servants, and stewards, who are to serve the rest in the ministry of the word, for teaching the faith of Christ and the liberty of believers. For though it is true that we are all equally priests, yet we cannot, nor, if we could, ought we all to, minister and teach publicly. Thus Paul says, "Let a man so account of us as of the ministers of Christ and stewards of the mysteries of God" (1 Cor. 4:1).

This bad system has now issued in such a pompous display of power and such a terrible tyranny that no earthly government can be compared to it, as if the laity were something else than Christians. Through this perversion of things it has happened that the knowledge of Christian grace, of faith, of liberty, and altogether of Christ, has utterly perished, and has been succeeded by an intolerable bondage to human works and laws; and, according to the Lamentations of Jeremiah, we have become the slaves of the vilest men on earth, who abuse our misery to all the disgraceful and ignominious purposes of their own will.

*****

Returning to the subject which we had begun, I think it is made clear by these considerations that it is not sufficient, nor a Christian course, to preach the works, life, and words of Christ in a historic manner, as facts which it suffices to know as an example how to frame our life, as do those who are now held the best preachers, and much less so to keep silence altogether on these things and to teach in their stead the laws of men and the decrees of the Fathers. There are now not a few persons who preach and read about Christ with the object of moving the human affections to sympathize with Christ, to indignation against the Jews, and other childish and womanish absurdities of that kind.

Now preaching ought to have the object of promoting faith in Him, so that He may not only be Christ, but a Christ for you and for me, and that what is said of Him, and what He is called, may work in us. And this faith is produced and is maintained by preaching why Christ came, what He has brought us and given to us, and to what profit and advantage He is to be received. This is done when the Christian liberty which we have from Christ Himself is rightly taught, and we are shown in what manner all we Christians are kings and priests, and how we are lords of all things, and may be confident that whatever we do in the presence of God is pleasing and acceptable to Him.

Whose heart would not rejoice in its inmost core at hearing these things? Whose heart, on receiving so great a consolation, would not become sweet with the love of Christ, a love to which it can never attain by any laws or works? Who can injure such a heart, or make it afraid? If the consciousness of sin or the horror of death rush in upon it, it is prepared to hope in the Lord, and is fearless of such evils, and undisturbed, until it shall look down upon its enemies. For it believes that the righteousness of Christ is its own, and that its sin is no longer its own, but that of Christ; but, on account of its faith in Christ, all its sin must needs be swallowed up from before the face of the righteousness of Christ, as I have said above. It learns, too, with the Apostle, to scoff at death and sin, and to say, "O death, where is thy sting? O grave, where is thy victory? The sting of death is sin, and the strength of sin is the law. But thanks be to God, which giveth us the victory through our Lord Jesus Christ" (1 Corinthians 15:55-57). For death is swallowed up in victory, not only the victory of Christ, but ours also, since by faith it becomes ours, and in it we too conquer.

Let it suffice to say this concerning the inner man and its liberty, and concerning that righteousness of faith which needs neither laws nor good works; nay, they are even hurtful to it, if any one pretends to be justified by them.

And now let us turn to the other part: to the outward man. Here we shall give an answer to all those who, taking offence at the word of faith and at what I have asserted, say, "If faith does everything, and by itself suffices for justification, why then are good works commanded? Are we then to take our ease and do no works, content with faith?" Not so, impious men, I reply; not so. That would indeed really be the case, if we were thoroughly and completely inner and spiritual persons; but that will not happen until the last day, when the dead shall be raised. As long as we live in the flesh, we are but beginning and making advances in that which shall be completed in a future life. On this account the Apostle calls that which we have in this life the first-fruits of the Spirit (Romans 8:23). In future we shall have the tenths, and the fullness of the Spirit. To this part belongs the fact I have stated before: that the Christian is the servant of all and subject to all. For in that part in which he is free he does no works, but in that in which he is a servant he does all works. Let us see on what principle this is so.

Although, as I have said, inwardly, and according to the spirit, a man is amply enough justified by faith, having all that he requires to have, except that this very faith and abundance ought to increase from day to day, even till the future life, still he remains in this mortal life upon earth, in which it is necessary that he should rule his own body and have intercourse with men. Here then works begin; here he must not take his ease; here he must give heed to exercise his body by fastings, watchings, labor, and other regular discipline, so that it may be subdued to the spirit, and obey and conform itself to the inner man and faith, and not rebel against them nor hinder them, as is its nature to do if it is not kept under. For the inner man, being conformed to God and created after the image of God through faith, rejoices and delights itself in Christ, in whom such blessings have been conferred on it, and hence has only this task before it: to serve God with joy and for nought in free love.

But in doing this he comes into collision with that contrary will in his own flesh, which is striving to serve the world and to seek its own gratification. This the spirit of faith cannot and will not bear, but applies itself with cheerfulness and zeal to keep it down and restrain it, as Paul says, "I delight in the law of God after the inward man; but I see another law in my members, warring against the law of my mind and bringing me into captivity to the law of sin" (Rom. 7:22-23), and again, "I keep under my body, and bring it unto subjection, lest that by any means, when I have preached to others, I myself should be a castaway" (1 Cor. 9:27), and "They that are Christ's have crucified the flesh, with the affections and lusts" (Gal. 5:24).

These works, however, must not be done with any notion that by them a man can be justified before God--for faith, which alone is righteousness before God, will not bear with this false notion--but solely with this purpose: that the body may be brought into subjection, and be purified from its evil lusts, so that our eyes may be turned only to purging away those lusts. For when the soul has been cleansed by faith and made to love God, it would have all things to be cleansed in like manner, and especially its own body, so that all things might unite with it in the love and praise of God. Thus it comes that, from the requirements of his own body, a man cannot take his ease, but is compelled on its account to do many good works, that he may bring it into subjection. Yet these works are not the means of his justification before God; he does them out of disinterested love to the service of God; looking to no other end than to do what is well-pleasing to Him whom he desires to obey most dutifully in all things.

On this principle every man may easily instruct himself in what measure, and with what distinctions, he ought to chasten his own body. He will fast, watch, and labor, just as much as he sees to suffice for keeping down the wantonness and concupiscence of the body. But those who pretend to be justified by works are looking, not to the mortification of their lusts, but only to the works themselves; thinking that, if they can accomplish as many works and as great ones as possible, all is well with them, and they are justified. Sometimes they even injure their brain, and extinguish nature, or at least make it useless. This is enormous folly, and ignorance of Christian life and faith, when a man seeks, without faith, to be justified and saved by works.

To make what we have said more easily understood, let us set it forth under a figure. The works of a Christian man, who is justified and saved by his faith out of the pure and free mercy of God, ought to be regarded in the same light as would have been those of Adam and Eve in paradise and of all their posterity if they had not sinned. Of them it is said, "The Lord God took the man and put him into the garden of Eden to dress it and to keep it" (Genesis 2:15). Now Adam had been created by God just and righteous, so that he could not have needed to be justified and made righteous by keeping the garden and working in it; but, that he might not be unemployed, God gave him the business of keeping and cultivating paradise. These would have indeed been works of perfect freedom, being done for no object but that of pleasing God, and not in order to obtain justification, which he already had to the full, and which would have been innate in us all.

So it is with the works of a believer. Being by his faith replaced afresh in paradise and created anew, he does not need works for his justification, but that he may not be idle, but may exercise his own body and preserve it. His works are to be done freely, with the sole object of pleasing God. Only we are not yet fully created anew in perfect faith and love; these require to be increased, not, however, through works, but through themselves.

A bishop, when he consecrates a church, confirms children, or performs any other duty of his office, is not consecrated as bishop by these works; nay, unless he had been previously consecrated as bishop, not one of those works would have any validity; they would be foolish, childish, and ridiculous. Thus a Christian, being consecrated by his faith, does good works; but he is not by these works made a more sacred person, or more a Christian. That is the effect of faith alone; nay, unless he were previously a believer and a Christian, none of his works would have any value at all; they would really be impious and damnable sins.

True, then, are these two sayings: "Good works do not make a good man, but a good man does good works"; "Bad works do not make a bad man, but a bad man does bad works." Thus it is always necessary that the substance or person should be good before any good works can be done, and that good works should follow and proceed from a good person. As Christ says, "A good tree cannot bring forth evil fruit, neither can a corrupt tree bring forth good fruit" (Matthew 8:18). Now it is clear that the fruit does not bear the tree, nor does the tree grow on the fruit; but, on the contrary, the trees bear the fruit, and the fruit grows on the trees.

As then trees must exist before their fruit, and as the fruit does not make the tree either good or bad, but on the contrary, a tree of either kind produces fruit of the same kind, so must first the person of the man be good or bad before he can do either a good or a bad work; and his works do not make him bad or good, but he himself makes his works either bad or good.

We may see the same thing in all handicrafts. A bad or good house does not make a bad or good builder, but a good or bad builder makes a good or bad house. And in general no work makes the workman such as it is itself; but the workman makes the work such as he is himself. Such is the case, too, with the works of men. Such as the man himself is, whether in faith or in unbelief, such is his work: good if it be done in faith; bad if in unbelief. But the converse is not true that, such as the work is, such the man becomes in faith or in unbelief. For as works do not make a believing man, so neither do they make a justified man; but faith, as it makes a man a believer and justified, so also it makes his works good.

Since then works justify no man, but a man must be justified before he can do any good work, it is most evident that it is faith alone which, by the mere mercy of God through Christ, and by means of His word, can worthily and sufficiently justify and save the person; and that a Christian man needs no work, no law, for his salvation; for by faith he is free from all law, and in perfect freedom does gratuitously all that he does, seeking nothing either of profit or of salvation--since by the grace of God he is already saved and rich in all things through his faith--but solely that which is well-pleasing to God.

So, too, no good work can profit an unbeliever to justification and salvation; and, on the other hand, no evil work makes him an evil and condemned person, but that unbelief, which makes the person and the tree bad, makes his works evil and condemned. Wherefore, when any man is made good or bad, this does not arise from his works, but from his faith or unbelief, as the wise man says, "The beginning of sin is to fall away from God"; that is, not to believe. Paul says, "He that cometh to God must believe" (Hebrews 11:6); and Christ says the same thing: "Either make the tree good and his fruit good; or else make the tree corrupt, and his fruit corrupt" (Matthew 7:33),--as much as to say, He who wishes to have good fruit will begin with the tree, and plant a good one; even so he who wishes to do good works must begin, not by working, but by believing, since it is this which makes the person good. For nothing makes the person good but faith, nor bad but unbelief.

It is certainly true that, in the sight of men, a man becomes good or evil by his works; but here "becoming" means that it is thus shown and recognized who is good or evil, as Christ says, "By their fruits ye shall know them" (Matthew 7:20). But all this stops at appearances and externals; and in this matter very many deceive themselves, when they presume to write and teach that we are to be justified by good works, and meanwhile make no mention even of faith, walking in their own ways, ever deceived and deceiving, going from bad to worse, blind leaders of the blind, wearying themselves with many works, and yet never attaining to true righteousness, of whom Paul says, "Having a form of godliness, but denying the power thereof, ever learning and never able to come to the knowledge of the truth" (2 Timothy 3:5, 7).

He then who does not wish to go astray, with these blind ones, must look further than to the works of the law or the doctrine of works; nay, must turn away his sight from works, and look to the person, and to the manner in which it may be justified. Now it is justified and saved, not by works or laws, but by the word of God--that is, by the promise of His grace--so that the glory may be to the Divine majesty, which has saved us who believe, not by works of righteousness which we have done, but according to His mercy, by the word of His grace.

From all this it is easy to perceive on what principle good works are to be cast aside or embraced, and by what rule all teachings put forth concerning works are to be understood. For if works are brought forward as grounds of justification, and are done under the false persuasion that we can pretend to be justified by them, they lay on us the yoke of necessity, and extinguish liberty along with faith, and by this very addition to their use they become no longer good, but really worthy of condemnation. For such works are not free, but blaspheme the grace of God, to which alone it belongs to justify and save through faith. Works cannot accomplish this, and yet, with impious presumption, through our folly, they take it on themselves to do so; and thus break in with violence upon the office and glory of grace.

We do not then reject good works; nay, we embrace them and teach them in the highest degree. It is not on their own account that we condemn them, but on account of this impious addition to them and the perverse notion of seeking justification by them. These things cause them to be only good in outward show, but in reality not good, since by them men are deceived and deceive others, like ravening wolves in sheep's clothing.

Now this leviathan, this perverted notion about works, is invincible when sincere faith is wanting. For those sanctified doers of works cannot but hold it till faith, which destroys it, comes and reigns in the heart. Nature cannot expel it by her own power; nay, cannot even see it for what it is, but considers it as a most holy will. And when custom steps in besides, and strengthens this depravity of nature, as has happened by means of impious teachers, then the evil is incurable, and leads astray multitudes to irreparable ruin. Therefore, though it is good to preach and write about penitence, confession, and satisfaction, yet if we stop there, and do not go on to teach faith, such teaching is without doubt deceitful and devilish. For Christ, speaking by His servant John, not only said, "Repent ye," but added, "for the kingdom of heaven is at hand" (Matthew 3:2).

For not one word of God only, but both, should be preached; new and old things should be brought out of the treasury, as well the voice of the law as the word of grace. The voice of the law should be brought forward, that men may be terrified and brought to a knowledge of their sins, and thence be converted to penitence and to a better manner of life. But we must not stop here; that would be to wound only and not to bind up, to strike and not to heal, to kill and not to make alive, to bring down to hell and not to bring back, to humble and not to exalt. Therefore the word of grace and of the promised remission of sin must also be preached, in order to teach and set up faith, since without that word contrition, penitence, and all other duties, are performed and taught in vain.

There still remain, it is true, preachers of repentance and grace, but they do not explain the law and the promises of God to such an end, and in such a spirit, that men may learn whence repentance and grace are to come. For repentance comes from the law of God, but faith or grace from the promises of God, as it is said, "Faith cometh by hearing, and hearing by the word of God" (Romans 10:17), whence it comes that a man, when humbled and brought to the knowledge of himself by the threatenings and terrors of the law, is consoled and raised up by faith in the Divine promise. Thus "weeping may endure for a night, but joy cometh in the morning" (Psalm 30:5). Thus much we say concerning works in general, and also concerning those which the Christian practices with regard to his own body.

*****

Lastly, we will speak also of those works which he performs towards his neighbor. For man does not live for himself alone in this mortal body, in order to work on its account, but also for all men on earth; nay, he lives only for others, and not for himself. For it is to this end that he brings his own body into subjection, that he may be able to serve others more sincerely and more freely, as Paul says, "None of us liveth to himself, and no man dieth to himself. For whether we live, we live unto the Lord; and whether we die, we die unto the Lord" (Romans 14:7, 8). Thus it is impossible that he should take his ease in this life, and not work for the good of his neighbors, since he must needs speak, act, and converse among men, just as Christ was made in the likeness of men and found in fashion as a man, and had His conversation among men.

Yet a Christian has need of none of these things for justification and salvation, but in all his works he ought to entertain this view and look only to this object--that he may serve and be useful to others in all that he does; having nothing before his eyes but the necessities and the advantage of his neighbor. Thus the Apostle commands us to work with our own hands, that we may have to give to those that need. He might have said, that we may support ourselves; but he tells us to give to those that need. It is the part of a Christian to take care of his own body for the very purpose that, by its soundness and well-being, he may be enabled to labor, and to acquire and preserve property, for the aid of those who are in want, that thus the stronger member may serve the weaker member, and we may be children of God, thoughtful and busy one for another, bearing one another's burdens, and so fulfilling the law of Christ.

Here is the truly Christian life, here is faith really working by love, when a man applies himself with joy and love to the works of that freest servitude in which he serves others voluntarily and for nought, himself abundantly satisfied in the fullness and riches of his own faith.

Thus, when Paul had taught the Philippians how they had been made rich by that faith in Christ in which they had obtained all

43

things, he teaches them further in these words: "If there be therefore any consolation in Christ, if any comfort of love, if any fellowship of the Spirit, if any bowels and mercies, fulfill ye my joy, that ye be like-minded, having the same love, being of one accord, of one mind. Let nothing be done through strife or vainglory; but in lowliness of mind let each esteem other better than themselves. Look not every man on his own things, but every man also on the things of others" (Philippians 2:1-4).

In this we see clearly that the Apostle lays down this rule for a Christian life: that all our works should be directed to the advantage of others, since every Christian has such abundance through his faith that all his other works and his whole life remain over and above wherewith to serve and benefit his neighbor of spontaneous goodwill.

To this end he brings forward Christ as an example, saying, "Let this mind be in you, which was also in Christ Jesus, who, being in the form of God, thought it not robbery to be equal with God, but made Himself of no reputation, and took upon Him the form of a servant, and was made in the likeness of men; and being found in fashion as a man, He humbled Himself, and became obedient unto death" (Philippians 2:5-8). This most wholesome saying of the Apostle has been darkened to us by men who, totally misunderstanding the expressions "form of God," "form of a servant," "fashion," "likeness of men," have transferred them to the natures of Godhead and manhood. Paul's meaning is this: Christ, when He was full of the form of God and abounded in all good things, so that He had no need of works or sufferings to be just and saved--for all these things He had from the very beginning--yet was not puffed up with these things, and did not raise Himself above us and arrogate to Himself power over us, though He might lawfully have done so, but, on the contrary, so acted in laboring, working, suffering, and dying, as to be like the rest of men, and no otherwise than a man in fashion and in conduct, as if He were in want of all things and had nothing of the form of God; and yet all this He did for our sakes, that He might serve us, and that all the works He should do under that form of a servant might become ours.

Thus a Christian, like Christ his Head, being full and in abundance through his faith, ought to be content with this form of God, obtained by faith; except that, as I have said, he ought to increase this faith till it be perfected. For this faith is his life, justification, and salvation, preserving his person itself and making it pleasing to God, and bestowing on him all that Christ has, as I have said above, and as Paul affirms: "The life which I now live in the flesh I live by the faith of the Son of God" (Galatians 2:20). Though he is thus free from all works, yet he ought to empty himself of this liberty, take on him the form of a servant, be made in the likeness of men, be found in fashion as a man, serve, help, and in every way act towards his neighbor as he sees that God through Christ has acted and is acting towards him. All this he should do freely, and with regard to nothing but the good pleasure of God, and he should reason thus:

Lo! my God, without merit on my part, of His pure and free mercy, has given to me, an unworthy, condemned, and contemptible creature all the riches of justification and salvation in Christ, so that I no longer am in want of anything, except of faith to believe that this is so. For such a Father, then, who has overwhelmed me with these inestimable riches of His, why should I not freely, cheerfully, and with my whole heart, and from voluntary zeal, do all that I know will be pleasing to Him and acceptable in His sight? I will therefore give myself as a sort of Christ, to my neighbor, as Christ has given Himself to me; and will do nothing in this life except what I see will be needful, advantageous, and wholesome for my neighbor, since by faith I abound in all good things in Christ.

Thus from faith flow forth love and joy in the Lord, and from love a cheerful, willing, free spirit, disposed to serve our neighbor voluntarily, without taking any account of gratitude or ingratitude, praise or blame, gain or loss. Its object is not to lay men under obligations, nor does it distinguish between friends and enemies, or look to gratitude or ingratitude, but most freely and willingly spends itself and its goods, whether it loses them through ingratitude, or gains goodwill. For thus did its Father, distributing all things to all men abundantly and freely,

45

making His sun to rise upon the just and the unjust. Thus, too, the child does and endures nothing except from the free joy with which it delights through Christ in God, the Giver of such great gifts.

You see, then, that, if we recognize those great and precious gifts, as Peter says, which have been given to us, love is quickly diffused in our hearts through the Spirit, and by love we are made free, joyful, all-powerful, active workers, victors over all our tribulations, servants to our neighbor, and nevertheless lords of all things. But, for those who do not recognize the good things given to them through Christ, Christ has been born in vain; such persons walk by works, and will never attain the taste and feeling of these great things. Therefore just as our neighbor is in want, and has need of our abundance, so we too in the sight of God were in want, and had need of His mercy. And as our heavenly Father has freely helped us in Christ, so ought we freely to help our neighbor by our body and works, and each should become to other a sort of Christ, so that we may be mutually Christs, and that the same Christ may be in all of us; that is, that we may be truly Christians.

Who then can comprehend the riches and glory of the Christian life? It can do all things, has all things, and is in want of nothing; is lord over sin, death, and hell, and at the same time is the obedient and useful servant of all. But alas! it is at this day unknown throughout the world; it is neither preached nor sought after, so that we are quite ignorant about our own name, why we are and are called Christians. We are certainly called so from Christ, who is not absent, but dwells among us--provided, that is, that we believe in Him and are reciprocally and mutually one the Christ of the other, doing to our neighbor as Christ does to us. But now, in the doctrine of men, we are taught only to seek after merits, rewards, and things which are already ours, and we have made of Christ a taskmaster far more severe than Moses.

The Blessed Virgin beyond all others, affords us an example of the same faith, in that she was purified according to the law of Moses, and like all other women, though she was bound by no such law and had no need of purification. Still she submitted to the law voluntarily and of free love, making herself like the rest of women, that she might not offend or throw contempt on them. She was not justified by doing this; but, being already justified, she did it freely and gratuitously. Thus ought our works too to be done, and not in order to be justified by them; for, being first justified by faith, we ought to do all our works freely and cheerfully for the sake of others.

St. Paul circumcised his disciple Timothy, not because he needed circumcision for his justification, but that he might not offend or contemn those Jews, weak in the faith, who had not yet been able to comprehend the liberty of faith. On the other hand, when they contemned liberty and urged that circumcision was necessary for justification, he resisted them, and would not allow Titus to be circumcised. For, as he would not offend or contemn any one's weakness in faith, but yielded for the time to their will, so, again, he would not have the liberty of faith offended or contemned by hardened self-justifiers, but walked in a middle path, sparing the weak for the time, and always resisting the hardened, that he might convert all to the liberty of faith. On the same principle we ought to act, receiving those that are weak in the faith, but boldly resisting these hardened teachers of works, of whom we shall hereafter speak at more length.

Christ also, when His disciples were asked for the tribute money, asked of Peter whether the children of a king were not free from taxes. Peter agreed to this; yet Jesus commanded him to go to the sea, saying, "Lest we should offend them, go thou to the sea, and cast a hook, and take up the fish that first cometh up; and when thou hast opened his mouth thou shalt find a piece of money; that take, and give unto them for Me and thee" (Matthew 17:27).

This example is very much to our purpose; for here Christ calls Himself and His disciples free men and children of a King, in want of nothing; and yet He voluntarily submits and pays the tax. Just as far, then, as this work was necessary or useful to Christ for justification or salvation, so far do all His other works or those of His disciples avail for justification. They are really free and subsequent to justification, and only done to serve others and set them an example.

Such are the works which Paul inculcated, that Christians should be subject to principalities and powers and ready to every good work (Titus 3:1), not that they may be justified by these things--for they are already justified by faith--but that in liberty of spirit they may thus be the servants of others and subject to powers, obeying their will out of gratuitous love.

Such, too, ought to have been the works of all colleges, monasteries, and priests; every one doing the works of his own profession and state of life, not in order to be justified by them, but in order to bring his own body into subjection, as an example to others, who themselves also need to keep under their bodies, and also in order to accommodate himself to the will of others, out of free love. But we must always guard most carefully against any vain confidence or presumption of being justified, gaining merit, or being saved by these works, this being the part of faith alone, as I have so often said.

Any man possessing this knowledge may easily keep clear of danger among those innumerable commands and precepts of the Pope, of bishops, of monasteries, of churches, of princes, and of magistrates, which some foolish pastors urge on us as being necessary for justification and salvation, calling them precepts of the Church, when they are not so at all. For the Christian freeman will speak thus: I will fast, I will pray, I will do this or that which is commanded me by men, not as having any need of these things for justification or salvation, but that I may thus comply with the will of the Pope, of the bishop, of such a community or such a magistrate, or of my neighbor as an example to him; for this cause I will do and suffer all things, just as Christ did and suffered much more for me, though He needed not at all to do so on His own account, and made Himself for my sake under the law, when He was not under the law. And although tyrants may do me violence or wrong in requiring obedience to these things, yet it will not hurt me to do them, so long as they are not done against God.

From all this every man will be able to attain a sure judgment and faithful discrimination between all works and laws, and to know who are blind and foolish pastors, and who are true and good ones. For whatsoever work is not directed to the sole end either of keeping under the body, or of doing service to our neighbor--provided he require nothing contrary to the will of God--is no good or Christian work. Hence I greatly fear that at this day few or no colleges, monasteries, altars, or ecclesiastical functions are Christian ones; and the same may be said of fasts and special prayers to certain saints. I fear that in all these nothing is being sought but what is already ours; while we fancy that by these things our sins are purged away and salvation is attained, and thus utterly do away with Christian liberty. This comes from ignorance of Christian faith and liberty.

This ignorance and this crushing of liberty are diligently promoted by the teaching of very many blind pastors, who stir up and urge the people to a zeal for these things, praising them and puffing them up with their indulgences, but never teaching faith. Now I would advise you, if you have any wish to pray, to fast, or to make foundations in churches, as they call it, to take care not to do so with the object of gaining any advantage, either temporal or eternal. You will thus wrong your faith, which alone bestows all things on you, and the increase of which, either by working or by suffering, is alone to be cared for. What you give, give freely and without price, that others may prosper and have increase from you and your goodness. Thus you will be a truly good man and a Christian. For what to you are your goods and your works, which are done over and above for the subjection of the body, since you have abundance for yourself through your faith, in which God has given you all things?

We give this rule: the good things which we have from God ought to flow from one to another and become common to all, so that every one of us may, as it were, put on his neighbor, and so behave towards him as if he were himself in his place. They flowed and do flow from Christ to us; He put us on, and acted for us as if He Himself were what we are. From us they flow to those who have need of them; so that my faith and righteousness ought to be laid down before God as a covering and intercession for the sins of my neighbor, which I am to take on myself, and so labor and endure servitude in them, as if they were my own; for thus has Christ done for us. This is true love and the genuine truth of Christian life. But only there is it true and genuine where there is true and genuine faith. Hence the Apostle attributes to charity this quality: that she seeketh not her own.

We conclude therefore that a Christian man does not live in himself, but in Christ and in his neighbor, or else is no Christian: in Christ by faith; in his neighbor by love. By faith he is carried upwards above himself to God, and by love he sinks back below himself to his neighbor, still always-abiding in God and His love, as Christ says, "Verily I say unto you, Hereafter ye shall see heaven open, and the angels of God ascending and descending upon the Son of man" (John 1:51).

Thus much concerning liberty, which, as you see, is a true and spiritual liberty, making our hearts free from all sins, laws, and commandments, as Paul says, "The law is not made for a righteous man" (1 Timothy 1:9), and one which surpasses all other external liberties, as far as heaven is above earth. May Christ make us to understand and preserve this liberty. Amen.

*****

Finally, for the sake of those to whom nothing can be stated so well but that they misunderstand and distort it, we must add a word, in case they can understand even that. There are very many persons who, when they hear of this liberty of faith, straightway turn it into an occasion of license. They think that everything is now lawful for them, and do not choose to show themselves free men and Christians in any other way than by their contempt and reprehension of ceremonies, of traditions, of human laws; as if they were Christians merely because they refuse to fast on stated days, or eat flesh when others fast, or omit the customary prayers; scoffing at the precepts of men, but utterly passing over all the rest that belongs to the Christian religion. On the other hand, they are most pertinaciously resisted by those who strive after salvation solely by their observance of and reverence for ceremonies, as if they would be saved merely because they fast on stated days, or abstain from flesh, or make formal prayers; talking loudly of the precepts of the Church and of the Fathers, and not caring a straw about those things which belong to our genuine faith. Both these parties are plainly culpable, in that, while they neglect matters which are of weight and necessary for salvation, they contend noisily about such as are without weight and not necessary.

How much more rightly does the Apostle Paul teach us to walk in the middle path, condemning either extreme and saying, "Let not him that eateth despise him that eateth not; and let not him which eateth not judge him that eateth" (Romans 14:3)! You see here how the Apostle blames those who, not from religious feeling, but in mere contempt, neglect and rail at ceremonial observances, and teaches them not to despise, since this "knowledge puffeth up." Again, he teaches the pertinacious upholders of these things not to judge their opponents. For neither party observes towards the other that charity which edifieth. In this matter we must listen to Scripture, which teaches us to turn aside neither to the right hand nor to the left, but to follow those right precepts of the Lord which rejoice the heart. For just as a man is not righteous merely because he serves and is devoted to works and ceremonial rites, so neither will he be accounted righteous merely because he neglects and despises them.

It is not from works that we are set free by the faith of Christ, but from the belief in works, that is from foolishly presuming to seek justification through works. Faith redeems our consciences, makes them upright, and preserves them, since by it we recognize the truth that justification does not depend on our works, although good works neither can nor ought to be absent, just as we cannot exist without food and drink and all the functions of this mortal body. Still it is not on them that our justification is based, but on faith; and yet they ought not on that account to be despised or neglected. Thus in this world we are compelled by the needs of this bodily life; but we are not hereby justified. "My kingdom is not hence, nor of this world," says Christ; but He does not say, "My kingdom is not here, nor in this world." Paul, too, says, "Though we walk in the flesh, we do not war after the flesh" (2 Corinthians 10:3), and "The life which I now live in the flesh I live by the faith of the Son of God" (Galatians 2:20). Thus our doings, life, and being, in works and ceremonies, are done from the necessities of this life, and with the motive of governing our bodies; but yet we are not justified by these things, but by the faith of the Son of God.

The Christian must therefore walk in the middle path, and set these two classes of men before his eyes. He may meet with hardened and obstinate ceremonialists, who, like deaf adders, refuse to listen to the truth of liberty, and cry up, enjoin, and urge on us their ceremonies, as if they could justify us without faith. Such were the Jews of old, who would not understand, that they might act well. These men we must resist, do just the contrary to what they do, and be bold to give them offence, lest by this impious notion of theirs they should deceive many along with themselves. Before the eyes of these men it is expedient to eat flesh, to break fasts, and to do in behalf of the liberty of faith things which they hold to be the greatest sins. We must say of them, "Let them alone; they be blind leaders of the blind" (Matthew 15:14). In this way Paul also would not have Titus circumcised, though these men urged it; and Christ defended the Apostles, who had plucked ears of corn on the Sabbath day; and many like instances.

Or else we may meet with simple-minded and ignorant persons, weak in the faith, as the Apostle calls them, who are as yet unable to apprehend that liberty of faith, even if willing to do so. These we must spare, lest they should be offended. We must bear with their infirmity, till they shall be more fully instructed. For since these men do not act thus from hardened malice, but only from weakness of faith, therefore, in order to avoid giving them offence, we must keep fasts and do other things which they consider necessary. This is required of us by charity, which injures no one, but serves all men. It is not the fault of these persons that they are weak, but that of their pastors, who by the snares and weapons of their own traditions have brought them into bondage and wounded their souls when they ought to have been set free and healed by the teaching of faith and liberty. Thus the Apostle says, "If meat make my brother to offend, I will eat no flesh while the world standeth" (1 Corinthians 8:13); and again, "I know, and am persuaded by the Lord Jesus, that there is nothing unclean of itself; but to him that esteemeth anything to be unclean, to him it is unclean. It is evil for that man who eateth with offence" (Romans 14:14, 20).

Thus, though we ought boldly to resist those teachers of tradition, and though the laws of the pontiffs, by which they make aggressions on the people of God, deserve sharp reproof, yet we must spare the timid crowd, who are held captive by the laws of those impious tyrants, till they are set free. Fight vigorously against the wolves, but on behalf of the sheep, not against the sheep. And this you may do by inveighing against the laws and lawgivers, and yet at the same time observing these laws with the weak, lest they be offended, until they shall themselves recognize the tyranny, and understand their own liberty. If you wish to use your liberty, do it secretly, as Paul says, "Hast thou faith? have it to thyself before God" (Romans 14:22). But take care not to use it in the presence of the weak. On the other hand, in the presence of tyrants and obstinate opposers, use your liberty in their despite, and with the utmost pertinacity, that they too may understand that they are tyrants, and their laws useless for justification, nay that they had no right to establish such laws.

Since then we cannot live in this world without ceremonies and works, since the hot and inexperienced period of youth has need of being restrained and protected by such bonds, and since everyone is bound to keep under his own body by attention to these things, therefore the minister of Christ must be prudent and faithful in so ruling and teaching the people of Christ, in all these matters, that no root of bitterness may spring up among them, and so many be defiled, as Paul warned the Hebrews; that is, that they may not lose the faith, and begin to be defiled by a belief in works as the means of justification. This is a thing which easily happens, and defiles very many, unless faith be constantly inculcated along with works. It is impossible to avoid this evil, when faith is passed over in silence, and only the ordinances of men are taught, as has been done hitherto by the pestilent, impious, and soul-destroying traditions of our pontiffs and opinions of our theologians. An infinite number of souls have been drawn down to hell by these snares, so that you may recognize the work of antichrist.

In brief, as poverty is imperiled amid riches, honesty amid business, humility amid honors, abstinence amid feasting, purity amid pleasures, so is justification by faith imperiled among ceremonies. Solomon says, "Can a man take fire in his bosom, and his clothes not be burned?" (Proverbs 6:27). And yet as we must live among riches, business, honors, pleasures, feastings, so must we among ceremonies, that is among perils. Just as infant boys have the greatest need of being cherished in the bosoms and by the care of girls, that they may not die, and yet, when they are grown, there is peril to their salvation in living among girls, so inexperienced and fervid young men require to be kept in and restrained by the barriers of ceremonies, even were they of iron, lest their weak minds should rush headlong into vice. And yet it would be death to them to persevere in believing that they can be justified by these things. They must rather be taught that they have been thus imprisoned, not with the purpose of their being justified or gaining merit in this way, but in order that they might avoid wrong-doing, and be more easily instructed in that righteousness which is by faith, a thing which the headlong character of youth would not bear unless it were put under restraint.

Hence in the Christian life ceremonies are to be no otherwise looked upon than as builders and workmen look upon those preparations for building or working which are not made with any view of being permanent or anything in themselves, but only because without them there could be no building and no work. When the structure is completed, they are laid aside. Here you see that we do not contemn these preparations, but set the highest value on them; a belief in them we do contemn, because no one thinks that they constitute a real and permanent structure. If anyone were so manifestly out of his senses as to have no other object in life but that of setting up these preparations with all possible expense, diligence, and perseverance, while he never thought of the structure itself, but pleased himself and made his boast of these useless preparations and props, should we not all pity his madness and think that, at the cost thus thrown away, some great building might have been raised?

Thus, too, we do not despise works and ceremonies--nay, we set the highest value on them; but we despise the belief in works, which no one should consider to constitute true righteousness, as do those hypocrites who employ and throw away their whole life in the pursuit of works, and yet never attain to that for the sake of which the works are done. As the Apostle says, they are "ever learning and never able to come to the knowledge of the truth" (2 Timothy 3:7). They appear to wish to build, they make preparations, and yet they never do build; and thus they continue in a show of godliness, but never attain to its power.

Meanwhile they please themselves with this zealous pursuit, and even dare to judge all others, whom they do not see adorned with such a glittering display of works; while, if they had been imbued with faith, they might have done great things for their own and others' salvation, at the same cost which they now waste in abuse of the gifts of God. But since human nature and natural reason, as they call it, are naturally superstitious, and quick to believe that justification can be attained by any laws or works proposed to them, and since nature is also exercised and confirmed in the same view by the practice of all earthly lawgivers, she can never of her own power free herself from this bondage to works, and come to a recognition of the liberty of faith.

We have therefore need to pray that God will lead us and make us taught of God, that is, ready to learn from God; and will Himself, as He has promised, write His law in our hearts; otherwise there is no hope for us. For unless He himself teach us inwardly this wisdom hidden in a mystery, nature cannot but condemn it and judge it to be heretical. She takes offence at it, and it seems folly to her, just as we see that it happened of old in the case of the prophets and Apostles, and just as blind and impious pontiffs, with their flatterers, do now in my case and that of those who are like me, upon whom, together with ourselves, may God at length have mercy, and lift up the light of His countenance upon them, that we may know His way upon earth and His saving health among all nations, who is blessed for evermore. Amen.

In the year of the Lord 1520.

A TREATISE ON GOOD WORKS

together with

THE LETTER OF DEDICATION

Dr. Martin Luther, 1520

DEDICATION

JESUS

To the Illustrious, High-born Prince and Lord, John Duke of Saxony, Landgrave of Thuringia, Margrave of Meissen, my gracious Lord and Patron.

Illustrious, High-born Prince, gracious Lord! My humble duty and my feeble prayer for your Grace always remembered!

For a long time, gracious Prince and Lord, I have wished to show my humble respect and duty toward your princely Grace, by the exhibition of some such spiritual wares as are at my disposal; but I have always considered my powers too feeble to undertake anything worthy of being offered to your princely Grace. Since, however, my most gracious Lord Frederick, Duke of Saxony, Elector and Vicar of the Holy Roman Empire, your Grace's brother, has not despised, but graciously accepted my slight book, dedicated to his electoral Grace, and now published--though such was not my intention, I have taken courage from his gracious example and ventured to think that the princely spirit, like the princely blood, may be the same in both of you, especially in gracious kindness and good will. I have hoped that your princely Grace likewise would not despise this my humble offering which I have felt more need of publishing than another of my sermons or tracts. For the greatest of all questions has been raised, the question of Good Works; in which is practiced immeasurably more trickery and deception than in anything else, and in which the simpleminded man is so easily misled that our Lord Christ has commanded us to watch carefully for the sheep's clothings under which the wolves hide themselves. Neither silver, gold, precious stones, nor any rare thing has such manifold alloys and flaws as have good works, which ought to have a single simple goodness, and without it are mere color, show and deceit. And although I know and daily hear many people, who think slightingly of my poverty, and say that I write only little pamphlets and German sermons for the unlearned laity, this shall not disturb me. Would to God I had in all my life, with all the ability I have, helped one layman to be better! I would be satisfied, thank God, and be quite willing then to let all my little books perish. Whether the making of many great books is an art and a benefit to the Church, I leave others to judge. But I believe that if I were minded to make great books according to their art, I could, with God's help, do it more readily perhaps than they could prepare a little discourse after my fashion. If accomplishment were as easy as persecution, Christ would long since have been cast out of heaven again, and God's throne itself overturned. Although we cannot all be writers, we all want to be critics. I will most gladly leave to anyone else the honor of greater things, and not be at all ashamed to preach and to write in German for the unlearned laymen. Although I too have little skill in it, I believe that if we had hitherto done, and should henceforth do more of it, Christendom would have reaped no small advantage, and have been more benefited by this than by the great, deep books and questions, which are used only in the schools, among the learned. Then, too, I have never forced or begged any one to hear me, or to read my sermons. I have freely ministered in the Church of that which God has given me and which I owe the Church. Whoever likes it not, may hear and read what others have to say. And if they are not willing to be my debtors, it matters little. For me it is enough, and even more than too much, that some laymen condescend to read what I say. Even though there were nothing else to urge me, it should be more than sufficient that I have learned that your princely Grace is pleased with such German books and is eager to receive instruction in Good Works and the Faith, with which instruction it was my duty, humbly and with all diligence to serve you. Therefore, in dutiful humility I pray that your princely Grace may accept this offering of mine with a gracious mind, until, if God grant me time, I prepare a German exposition of the Faith in its entirety. For at this time I have wished to show how in all good works we should practice and make use of faith, and let faith be the chief work. If God permit, I will treat at another time of the Faith itself--how we are daily to pray or recite it.

I humbly commend myself herewith to your princely Grace, Your Princely Grace's Humble Chaplain,

DR. MARTIN LUTHER.
From Wittenberg, March 29th, A. D. 1520

THE TREATISE

1. We ought first to know that there are no good works except those which God has commanded, even as there is no sin except that which God has forbidden. Therefore whoever wishes to know and to do good works needs nothing else than to know God's commandments. Thus Christ says, in Matthew 19, "If thou wilt enter into life, keep the commandments." And when the young man asks Him, also in Matthew 19, what he shall do that he may inherit eternal life, Christ sets before him naught else but the Ten Commandments. Accordingly, we must learn how to distinguish among good works from the Commandments of God, and not from the appearance, the magnitude, or the number of the works themselves, nor from the judgment of men or of human law or custom, as we see has been done and still is done, because we are blind and despise the divine Commandments.

2. The first and highest, the most precious of all good works is faith in Christ, as He says in John chapter 6. When the Jews asked Him: "What shall we do that we may work the works of God?" He answered: "This is the work of God, that ye believe on Him Whom He hath sent." When we hear or preach this word, we hasten over it and deem it a very little thing and easy to do, whereas we ought here to pause a long time and to ponder it well. For in this work all good works must be done and receive from it the inflow of their goodness, like a loan. This we must put bluntly, that men may understand it.

We find many who pray, fast, establish endowments, do this or that, lead a good life before men, and yet if you should ask them whether they are sure that what they do pleases God, they say, "No"; they do not know, or they doubt. And there are some very learned men, who mislead them, and say that it is not necessary to be sure of this; and yet, on the other hand, these same men do nothing else but teach good works. Now all these works are done outside of faith, therefore they are nothing and altogether dead. For as their conscience stands toward God and as it believes, so also are the works which grow out of it. Now they have no faith, no good conscience toward God, therefore the works lack their head, and all their life and goodness is nothing. Hence it comes that when I exalt faith and reject such works done without faith, they accuse me of forbidding good works, when in truth I am trying hard to teach real good works of faith.

3. If you ask further, whether they count it also a good work when they work at their trade, walk, stand, eat, drink, sleep, and do all kinds of works for the nourishment of the body or for the common welfare, and whether they believe that God takes pleasure in them because of such works, you will find that they say, "No"; and they define good works so narrowly that they are made to consist only of praying in church, fasting, and almsgiving. Other works they consider to be in vain, and think that God cares nothing for them. So through their damnable unbelief they curtail and lessen the service of God, Who is served by all things whatsoever that are done, spoken or thought in faith.

So teaches Ecclesiastes 9: "Go thy way with joy, eat and drink, and know that God accepteth thy works. Let thy garments be always white; and let thy head lack no ointment. Live joyfully with the wife whom thou lovest all the days of the life of thy vanity." "Let thy garments be always white," that is, let all our works be good, whatever they may be, without any distinction. And they are white when I am certain and believe that they please God. Then shall the head of my soul never lack the ointment of a joyful conscience.

So Christ says in John chapter 8: "I do always those things that please Him." And St. John says in 1 John chapter 3: "Hereby we know that we are of the truth, if we can comfort our hearts before Him and have a good confidence. And if our heart condemns or frets us, God is greater than our heart, and we have confidence, that whatsoever we ask, we shall receive of Him, because we keep His Commandments, and do those things that are pleasing in His sight." Again: "Whosoever is born of God, that is, whoever believes and trusts God, doth not commit sin, and cannot sin." Again, in Psalm 34: "None of them that trust in Him shall do sin." And in Psalm 2: "Blessed are all they that put their trust in Him." If this be true, then all that they do must be good, or the evil that they do must be quickly forgiven. Behold, then, why I exalt faith so greatly, draw all works into it, and reject all works which do not flow from it.

4. Now everyone can note and tell for himself when he does what is good or what is not good; for if he finds his heart confident that it pleases God, the work is good, even if it were so small a thing as picking up a straw. If confidence is absent, or if he doubts, the work is not good, although it should raise all the dead and the man should give himself to be burned. This is the teaching of St. Paul in Romans chapter 14: "Whatsoever is not done of or in faith is sin." Faith, as the chief work, and no other work, has given us the name of "believers on Christ." For all other works a heathen, a Jew, a Turk, a sinner, may also do; but to trust firmly that he pleases God, is possible only for a Christian who is enlightened and strengthened by grace.

That these words seem strange, and that some call me a heretic because of them, is due to the fact that men have followed blind reason and heathen ways, have set faith not above, but beside other virtues, and have given it a work of its own, apart from all works of the other virtues; although faith alone makes all other works good, acceptable and worthy, in that it trusts God and does not doubt that for it all things that a man does are well done. Indeed, they have not let faith remain a work, but have made a habit of it, as they say, although Scripture gives the name of a good, divine work to no work except to faith alone. Therefore it is no wonder that they have become blind and leaders of the blind. And this faith brings with it at once love, peace, joy and hope. For God gives His Spirit at once to him who trusts Him, as St. Paul says to the Galatians: "You received the Spirit not because of your good works, but when you believed the Word of God."

5. In this faith all works become equal, and one is like the other; all distinctions between works fall away, whether they be great, small, short, long, few or many. For the works are acceptable not for their own sake, but because of the faith which alone is, works and lives in each and every work without distinction, however numerous and various they are, just as all the members of the body live, work and have their name from the head, and without the head no member can live, work and have a name.

From which it further follows that a Christian who lives in this faith has no need of a teacher of good works, but whatever he finds to do he does, and all is well done; as Samuel said to Saul: "The Spirit of the Lord will come upon thee, and thou shalt be turned into another man; then do thou as occasion serves thee; for God is with thee." So also we read of St. Anna, Samuel's mother: "When she believed the priest Eli who promised her God's grace, she went home in joy and peace, and from that time no more turned hither and thither," that is, whatever occurred, it was all one to her. St. Paul also says: "Where the Spirit of Christ is, there all is free." For faith does not permit itself to be bound to any work, nor does it allow any work to be taken from it, but, as the First Psalm says, "He bringeth forth his fruit in his season," that is, as a matter of course.

6. This we may see in a common human example. When a man and a woman love and are pleased with each other, and thoroughly believe in their love, who teaches them how they are to behave, what they are to do, leave undone, say, not say, think? Confidence alone

teaches them all this, and more. They make no difference in works: they do the great, the long, the much, as gladly as the small, the short, the little, and vice versa; and that too with joyful, peaceful, confident hearts, and each is a free companion of the other. But where there is a doubt, search is made for what is best; then a distinction of works is imagined whereby a man may win favor; and yet he goes about it with a heavy heart, and great disrelish; he is, as it were, taken captive, more than half in despair, and often makes a fool of himself.

So a Christian who lives in this confidence toward God, a knows all things, can do all things, undertakes all things that are to be done, and does everything cheerfully and freely; not that he may gather many merits and good works, but because it is a pleasure for him to please God thereby, and he serves God purely for nothing, content that his service pleases God. On the other hand, he who is not at one with God, or doubts, hunts and worries in what way he may do enough and with many works move God. He runs to St. James of Compostella, to Rome, to Jerusalem, hither and yon, prays St. Bridget's prayer and the rest, fasts on this day and on that, makes confession here, and makes confession there, questions this man and that, and yet finds no peace. He does all this with great effort, despair and disrelish of heart, so that the Scriptures rightly call such works in Hebrew *Avenama*, that is, labor and travail. And even then they are not good works, and are all lost. Many have been crazed thereby; their fear has brought them into all manner of misery. Of these it is written in Wisdom of Solomon 5: "We have wearied ourselves in the wrong way; and have gone through deserts, where there lay no way; but as for the way of the Lord, we have not known it, and the sun of righteousness rose not upon us."

7. In these works faith is still slight and weak; let us ask further, whether they believe that they are well-pleasing to God when they suffer in body, property, honor, friends, or whatever they have, and believe that God of His mercy appoints their sufferings and difficulties for them, whether they be small or great. This is real strength, to trust

in God when to all our senses and reason He appears to be angry; and to have greater confidence in Him than we feel. Here He is hidden, as the bride says in the Song of Songs: "Behold he standeth behind our wall, he looketh forth at the windows"; that is, He stands hidden among the sufferings, which would separate us from Him like a wall, yea, like a wall of stone, and yet He looks upon me and does not leave me, for He is standing and is ready graciously to help, and through the window of dim faith He permits Himself to be seen. And Jeremiah says in Lamentations, "He casts off men, but He does it not willingly."

This faith they do not know at all, and give up, thinking that God has forsaken them and is become their enemy; they even lay the blame of their ills on men and devils, and have no confidence at all in God. For this reason, too, their suffering is always an offence and harmful to them, and yet they go and do some good works, as they think, and are not aware of their unbelief. But they who in such suffering trust God and retain a good, firm confidence in Him, and believe that He is pleased with them, these see in their sufferings and afflictions nothing but precious merits and the rarest possessions, the value of which no one can estimate. For faith and confidence make precious before God all that which others think most shameful, so that it is written even of death in Psalm 116:15, "Precious in the sight of the Lord is the death of His saints." And just as the confidence and faith are better, higher and stronger at this stage than in the first stage, so and to the same degree do the sufferings which are borne in this faith excel all works of faith. Therefore between such works and sufferings there is an immeasurable difference and the sufferings are infinitely better.

8. Beyond all this is the highest stage of faith, when; God punishes the conscience not only with temporal sufferings, but with death, hell, and sin, and refuses grace and mercy, as though it were His will to condemn and to be angry eternally. This few men experience, but David cries out in Psalm 6, "O Lord, rebuke me not in Thine anger."

To believe at such times that God, in His mercy, is pleased with us, is the highest work that can be done by and in the creature; but of this the work-righteous and doers of good works know nothing at all. For how could they here look for good things and grace from God, as long as they are not certain in their works, and doubt even on the lowest step of faith.

In this way I have, as I said, always praised faith, and rejected all works which are done without such faith, in order thereby to lead men from the false, pretentious, pharisaic, unbelieving good works, with which all monastic houses, churches, homes, low and higher classes are overfilled, and lead them to the true, genuine, thoroughly good, believing works. In this no one opposes me except the unclean beasts, which do not divide the hoof, as the Law of Moses decrees; who will suffer no distinction among good works, but go lumbering along: if only they pray, fast, establish endowments, go to confession, and do enough, everything shall be good, although in all this they have had no faith in God's grace and approval. Indeed, they consider the works best of all, when they have done many, great and long works without any such confidence, and they look for good only after the works are done; and so they build their confidence not on divine favor, but on the works they have done, that is, on sand and water, from which they must at last take a cruel fall, as Christ says in Matthew 7. This good-will and favor, on which our confidence rests, was proclaimed by the angels from heaven, when they sang on Christmas night: "*Gloria in excelsis Deo*, Glory to God in the highest, peace to earth, gracious favor to man."

9. Now this is the work of the First Commandment, which commands: "Thou shalt have no other gods," which means: "Since I alone am God, thou shalt place all thy confidence, trust and faith on Me alone, and on no one else." For that is not to have a god, if you call him God only with your lips, or worship him with the knees or bodily gestures; but if you trust Him with the heart, and look to Him

67

for all good, grace and favor, whether in works or sufferings, in life or death, in joy or sorrow; as the Lord Christ says to the heathen woman, John iv: "I say unto thee, they that worship God must worship Him in spirit and in truth." And this faith, faithfulness, confidence deep in the heart, is the true fulfilling of the First Commandment; without this there is no other work that is able to satisfy this Commandment. And as this Commandment is the very first, highest and best, from which all the others proceed, in which they exist, and by which they are directed and measured, so also its work, that is, the faith or confidence in God's favor at all times, is the very first, highest and best, from which all others must proceed, exist, remain, be directed and measured. Compared with this, other works are just as if the other Commandments were without the First, and there were no God, Therefore St. Augustine well says that the works of the First Commandment are faith, hope and love. As I said above, such faith and confidence bring love and hope with them. Nay, if we see it aright, love is the first, or comes at the same instant with faith. For I could not trust God, if I did not think that He wished to be favorable and to love me, which leads me, in turn, to love Him and to trust Him heartily and to look to Him for all good things.

10. Now you see for yourself that all those who do not at all times trust God and do not in all their works or sufferings, life and death, trust in His favor, grace and good-will, but seek His favor in other things or in themselves, do not keep this Commandment, and practice real idolatry, even if they were to do the works of all the other Commandments, and in addition had all the prayers, fasting, obedience, patience, chastity, and innocence of all the saints combined. For the chief work is not present, without which all the others are nothing but mere sham, show and pretence, with nothing back of them; against which Christ warns us in Matthew 7: "Beware of false prophets, which come to you in sheep's clothing." Such are all who wish with their many good works, as they say, to make God favorable to themselves, and to buy God's grace from Him, as if He were a huckster or a day-laborer, unwilling to give His grace and favor for nothing. These are the most perverse people on earth, who will hardly or never be converted to the right way. Such too are all who in adversity run hither and thither, and look for counsel and help everywhere except from God, from Whom they are most urgently commanded to seek it; whom the Prophet Isaiah reproves thus, in Isaiah 9: "The mad people turneth not to Him that smiteth them"; that is, God smote them and sent them sufferings and all kinds of adversity, that they should run to Him and trust Him. But they run away from Him to men, now to Egypt, now to Assyria, perchance also to the devil; and of such idolatry much is written in the same Prophet and in the Books of the Kings. This is also the way of all holy hypocrites when they are in trouble: they do not run to God, but flee from Him, and only think of how they may get rid of their trouble through their own efforts or through human help, and yet they consider themselves and let others consider them pious people.

11. This is what St. Paul means in many places, where he ascribes so much to faith, that he says: *Justus ex fide sua vivit*, "the righteous man draws his life out of his faith," and faith is that because of which he is counted righteous before God. If righteousness consists of faith,

it is clear that faith fulfils all commandments and makes all works righteous, since no one is justified except he keep all the commands of God. Again, the works can justify no one before God without faith. So utterly and roundly does the Apostle reject works and praise faith, that some have taken offence at his words and say: "Well, then, we will do no more good works," although he condemns such men as erring and foolish.

So men still do. When we reject the great, pretentious works of our time, which are done entirely without faith, they say: Men are only to believe and not to do anything good. For nowadays they say that the works of the First Commandment are singing, reading, organ-playing, reading the mass, saying matins and vespers and the other hours, the founding and decorating of churches, altars, and monastic houses, the gathering of bells, jewels, garments, trinkets and treasures, running to Rome and to the saints. Further, when we are dressed up and bow, kneel, pray the rosary and the Psalter, and all this not before an idol, but before the holy cross of God or the pictures of His saints: this we call honoring and worshiping God, and, according to the First Commandment, "having no other gods"; although these things usurers, adulterers and all manner of sinners can do too, and do them daily.

Of course, if these things are done with such faith that we believe that they please God, then they are praiseworthy, not because of their virtue, but because of such faith, for which all works are of equal value, as has been said. But if we doubt or do not believe that God is gracious to us and is pleased with us, or if we presumptuously expect to please Him only through and after our works, then it is all pure deception, outwardly honoring God, but inwardly setting up self as a false god. This is the reason why I have so often spoken against the display, magnificence and multitude of such works and have rejected them, because it is as clear as day that they are not only done in doubt or without faith, but there is not one in a thousand who does not set his confidence upon the works, expecting by them to win God's favor and anticipate His grace; and so they make a fair of them, a thing which God cannot endure, since He has promised His grace freely, and wills that we begin by trusting that grace, and in it perform all works, whatever they may be.

12. Note for yourself, then, how far apart these two are: keeping the First Commandment with outward works only, and keeping it with inward trust. For this last makes true, living children of God, the other only makes worse idolatry and the most mischievous hypocrites on earth, who with their apparent righteousness lead unnumbered people into their way, and yet allow them to be without faith, so that they are miserably misled, and are caught in the pitiable babbling and mummery. Of such Christ says in Matthew 24: "Beware, if any man shall say unto you, Lo, here is Christ, or there"; and in John chapter 4: "I say unto thee, the hour cometh, when ye shall neither in this mountain nor yet at Jerusalem worship God, for the Father seeketh spiritual worshipers."

These and similar passages have moved me and ought to move everyone to reject the great display of bulls, seals, flags, indulgences, by which the poor folk are led to build churches, to give, to endow, to pray, and yet faith is not mentioned, and is even suppressed. For since faith knows no distinction among works, such exaltation and urging of one work above another cannot exist beside faith. For faith desires to be the only service of God, and will grant this name and honor to no other work, except in so far as faith imparts it, as it does when the work is done in faith and by faith. This perversion is indicated in the Old Testament, when the Jews left the Temple and sacrificed at other places, in the green parks and on the mountains. This is what these men also do: they are zealous to do all works, but this chief work of faith they regard not at all.

13. Where now are they who ask, what works are good; what they shall do; how they shall be religious? Yes, and where are they who say

that when we preach of faith, we shall neither teach nor do works? Does not this First Commandment give us more work to do than any man can do? If a man were a thousand men, or all men, or all creatures, this Commandment would yet ask enough of him, and more than enough, since he is commanded to live and walk at all times in faith and confidence toward God, to place such faith in no one else, and so to have only one, the true God, and none other.

Now, since the being and nature of man cannot for an instant be without doing or not doing something, enduring or running away from something (for, as we see, life never rests), let him who will be pious and filled with good works, begin and in all his life and works at all times exercise himself in this faith; let him learn to do and to leave undone all things in such continual faith; then will he find how much work he has to do, and how completely all things are included in faith; how he dare never grow idle, because his very idling must be the exercise and work of faith. In brief, nothing can be in or about us and nothing can happen to us but that it must be good and meritorious, if we believe (as we ought) that all things please God. So says St. Paul: "Dear brethren, all that ye do, whether ye eat or drink, do all in the Name of Jesus Christ, our Lord." Now it cannot be done in this Name except it be done in this faith. Likewise, as Romans 7 says: "We know that all things work together for good to the saints of God."

Therefore, when some say that good works are forbidden when we preach faith alone, it is as if I said to a sick man: "If you had health, you would have the use of all your limbs; but without health, the works of all your limbs are nothing"; and he wanted to infer that I had forbidden the works of all his limbs; whereas, on the contrary, I meant that he must first have health, which will work all the works of all the members. So faith also must be in all works the master-workman and captain, or they are nothing at all.

14. You might say: "Why then do we have so many laws of the Church and of the State, and many ceremonies of churches, monastic

houses, holy places, which urge and tempt men to good works, if faith does all things through the First Commandment?" I answer: Simply because we do not all have faith or do not heed it. If every man had faith, we would need no more laws, but everyone would of himself at all times do good works, as his confidence in God teaches him.

But now there are four kinds of men: the first, just mentioned, who need no law, of whom St. Paul says in 1 Timothy 1, "The law is not made for a righteous man," that is, for the believer, but believers of themselves do what they know and can do, only because they firmly trust that God's favor and grace rests upon them in all things. The second class want to abuse this freedom, put a false confidence in it, and grow lazy; of whom St. Peter says in 1 Peter 2, "Ye shall live as free men, but not using your liberty for a cloak of maliciousness," as if he said: The freedom of faith does not permit sins, nor will it cover them, but it sets us free to do all manner of good works and to endure all things as they happen to us, so that a man is not bound only to one work or to a few. So also St. Paul, in Galatians 5 says: "Use not your liberty for an occasion to the flesh." Such men must be urged by laws and hemmed in by teaching and exhortation. The third class are wicked men, always ready for sins; these must be constrained by spiritual and temporal laws, like wild horses and dogs, and where this does not help, they must be put to death by the worldly sword, as St. Paul says in Romans 13: "The worldly ruler bears the sword, and serves God with it, not as a terror to the good, but to the evil." The fourth class, who are still lusty, and childish in their understanding of faith and of the spiritual life, must be coaxed like young children and tempted with external, definite and prescribed decorations, with reading, praying, fasting, singing, adorning of churches, organ playing, and such other things as are commanded and observed in monastic houses and churches, until they also learn to know the faith. Although there is great danger here, when the rulers, as is now, alas! the case, busy themselves with and insist upon such ceremonies and external works as if they were the true works, and neglect faith, which they ought always to teach along with these works, just as a mother gives her child other food along with the milk, until the child can eat the strong food by itself.

15. Since, then, we are not all alike, we must tolerate such people, share their observances and burdens, and not despise them, but teach them the true way of faith. So St. Paul teaches in Romans 14: "Him that is weak in the faith receive ye, to teach him." And so he did himself in 1 Corinthians 9: "To them that are under the law, I became as under the law, although I was not under the law." And Christ, in Matthew 17, when He was asked to pay tribute, which He was not obligated to pay, argues with St. Peter, whether the children of kings must give tribute, or only other people. St. Peter answers: "Only other people." Christ said: "Then are the children of kings free; notwithstanding, lest we should offend them, go thou to the sea, and cast an hook, and take up the fish that first cometh up; and in his mouth thou shalt find a piece of money; take that and give it for me and thee."

Here we see that all works and things are free to a Christian through his faith; and yet, because the others do not yet believe, he observes and bears with them what he is not obligated to do. But this he does freely, for he is certain that this is pleasing to God, and he does it willingly, accepts it as any other free work which comes to his hand without his choice, because he desires and seeks no more than that he may in his faith do works to please God.

But since in this discourse we have undertaken to teach what righteous and good works are, and are now speaking of the highest work, it is clear that we do not speak of the second, third and fourth classes of men, but of the first, into whose likeness all the others are to grow, and until they do so the first class must endure and instruct them. Therefore we must not despise, as if they were hopeless, these men of weak faith, who would gladly do right and learn, and yet cannot understand because of the ceremonies to which they cling; we must rather blame their ignorant, blind teachers, who have never taught them the faith, and have led them so deeply into works. They must be gently and gradually led back again to faith, as a sick man is treated, and must be allowed for a time, for their conscience sake, to cling to some works and do them as necessary to salvation, so long as they rightly grasp the faith; lest if we try to tear them out so suddenly, their weak consciences be quite shattered and confused, and retain neither faith nor works. But the hardheaded, who, hardened in their works, give no heed to what is said of faith, and fight against it, these we must, as Christ did and taught, let go their way, that the blind may lead the blind.

16. But you say: How can I trust surely that all my works are pleasing to God, when at times I fall, and talk, eat, drink and sleep too much, or otherwise transgress, as I cannot help doing? Answer: This question shows that you still regard faith as a work among other works, and do not set it above all works. For it is the highest work for this very reason, because it remains and blots out these daily sins by not doubting that God is so kind to you as to wink at such daily transgression and weakness. Aye, even if a deadly sin should occur (which, however, never or rarely happens to those who live in faith and trust toward God), yet faith rises again and does not doubt that its sin is already gone; as it is written I. John ii: "My little children, these things I write unto you, that ye sin not. And if any man sin, we have an Advocate with God the Father, Jesus Christ, Who is the propitiation of all our sins." And Wisdom 15: "For if we sin, we are Thine, knowing Thy power." And Proverbs 24 "For a just man falleth seven times, and riseth up again." Yes, this confidence and faith must be so high and strong that the man knows that all his life and works are nothing but damnable sins before God's judgment, as it is written in Psalm 143:2: "In thy sight shall no man living be justified"; and he must entirely despair of his works, believing that they cannot be good except through this faith, which looks for no judgment, but only for pure grace, favor, kindness and mercy, like David, Psalm 26: "Thy loving kindness is ever before mine eyes, and I have trusted in Thy truth"; Psalm 4: "The light of Thy countenance is lift up upon us (that is, the knowledge of Thy grace through faith), and thereby hast Thou put gladness in my heart"; for as faith trusts, so it receives.

See, thus are works forgiven, are without guilt and are good, not by their own nature, but by the mercy and grace of God because of the faith which trusts on the mercy of God. Therefore we must fear because of the works, but comfort ourselves because of the grace of God, as it is written in Psalm 147: "The Lord taketh pleasure in them that I fear Him, in those that hope in His mercy." So we pray with perfect confidence: "Our Father," and yet petition: "Forgive us our trespasses"; we are children and yet sinners; are acceptable and yet do not do enough; and all this is the work of faith, firmly grounded in God's grace.

17. But if you ask, where the faith and the confidence can be found and whence they come, this it is certainly most necessary to know. First: Without doubt faith does not come from your works or merit, but alone from Jesus Christ, and is freely promised and given; as St. Paul writes in Romans 5: "God commendeth His love to us as exceeding sweet and kindly, in that, while we were yet sinners, Christ died for us"; as if he said: "Ought not this give us a strong unconquerable confidence, that before we prayed or cared for it, yes, while we still continually walked in sins, Christ dies for our sin?" St. Paul concludes: "If while we were yet sinners Christ died for us, how much more then, being justified by His blood, shall we be saved from wrath through Him; and if, when we were enemies, we were reconciled to God by the death of His Son, much more, being reconciled, shall we be saved by His life."

Lo! thus must thou form Christ within thyself and see how in Him God holds before thee and offers thee His mercy without any previous merits of thine own, and from such a view of His grace must thou draw faith and confidence of the forgiveness of all thy sins. Faith, therefore, does not begin with works, neither do they create it, but it must spring up and flow from the blood, wounds and death of Christ. If thou see in these that God is so kindly affectioned toward thee that He gives even His Son for thee, then thy heart also must in its turn grow sweet and kindly affectioned toward God, and so thy confidence must grow out of pure good-will and love--God's love toward thee and thine toward God. We never read that the Holy Spirit was given to any one when he did works, but always when men have heard the Gospel of Christ and the mercy of God. From this same Word and from no other source must faith still come, even in our day and always. For Christ is the rock out of which men suck oil and honey, as Moses says in Deuteronomy chapter 32.

18. So far we have treated of the first work and of the First Commandment, but very briefly, plainly and hastily, for very much might be said of it. We will now trace the works farther through the following Commandments.

The second work, next to faith, is the work of the Second Commandment, that we shall honor God's Name and not take it in vain. This, like all the other works, cannot be done without faith; and if it is done without faith, it is all sham and show. After faith we can do no greater work than to praise, preach, sing and in every way exalt and magnify God's glory, honor and Name.

And although I have said above, and it is true, that there is no difference in works where faith is and does the work, yet this is true only when they are compared with faith and its works. Measured by one another there is a difference, and one is higher than the other. Just as in the body the members do not differ when compared with health, and health works in the one as much as in the other; yet the works of the members are different, and one is higher, nobler, more useful than the other; so, here also, to praise God's glory and Name is better than the works of the other Commandments which follow; and yet it must be done in the same faith as all the others.

But I know well that this work is lightly esteemed, and has indeed become unknown. Therefore we must examine it further, and will say no more about the necessity of doing it in the faith and confidence that it pleases God. Indeed there is no work in which confidence and faith are so much experienced and felt as in honoring God's Name; and it greatly helps to strengthen and increase faith, although all works also help to do this, as St. Peter says, 2 Peter 1 "Wherefore the rather, brethren, give diligence through good works to make your calling and election sure."

19. The First Commandment forbids us to have other gods, and thereby commands that we have a God, the true God, by a firm faith, trust, confidence, hope and love, which are the only works whereby a man can have, honor and keep a God; for by no other work can one find or lose God except by faith or unbelief, by trusting or doubting; of the other works none reaches quite to God. So also in the Second Commandment we are forbidden to use His Name in vain. Yet this is not to be enough, but we are thereby also commanded to honor, call upon, glorify, preach and praise His Name. And indeed it is impossible that God's Name should not be dishonored where it is not rightly honored. For although it be honored with the lips, bending of the knees, kissing and other postures, if this is not done in the heart by faith, in confident trust in God's grace, it is nothing else than an evidence and badge of hypocrisy.

See now, how many kinds of good works a man can do under this Commandment at all times and never be without the good works of this Commandment, if he will; so that he truly need not make a long pilgrimage or seek holy places. For, tell me, what moment can pass in which we do not without ceasing receive God's blessings, or, on the other hand, suffer adversity? But what else are God's blessings and adversities than a constant urging and stirring up to praise, honor, and bless God, and to call upon His Name? Now if you had nothing else at all to do, would you not have enough to do with this Commandment alone, that you without ceasing bless, sing, praise and honor God's Name? And for what other purpose have tongue, voice, language and mouth been created? As Psalm 51 says: "Lord, open Thou my lips, and my mouth shall show forth Thy praise." Again: "My tongue shall sing aloud of Thy mercy."

What work is there in heaven except that of this Second Commandment? As it is written in Psalm 84:4: "Blessed are they that dwell in Thy house: they will be forever praising Thee." So also David says in Psalm 34: "God's praise shall be continually in my mouth." And St. Paul, 1 Corinthians 10: "Whether therefore ye eat or drink, or whatsoever ye do, do all to the glory of God." Also Colossians 3: "Whatsoever ye do in word or deed, do all in the Name of the Lord Jesus, giving thanks to God and the Father." If we were to observe this work, we would have a heaven here on earth and always have enough to do, as have the saints in heaven.

20. On this is based the wonderful and righteous judgment of God, that at times a poor man, in whom no one can see many great works, in the privacy of his home joyfully praises God when he fares well, or with entire confidence calls upon Him when he fares ill, and thereby does a greater and more acceptable work than another, who fasts much, prays much, endows churches, makes pilgrimages, and burdens himself with great deeds in this place and in that. Such a fool opens wide his mouth, looks for great works to do, and is so blinded that he does not at all notice this greatest work, and praising God is in his eyes a very small matter compared with the great idea he has formed of the works of his own devising, in which he perhaps praises himself more than God, or takes more pleasure in them than he does in God; and thus with his good works he storms against the Second Commandment and its works. Of all this we have an illustration in the case of the Pharisee and the Publican in the Gospel. For the sinner calls upon God in his sins, and praises Him, and so has hit upon the two highest Commandments, faith and God's honor. The hypocrite misses both and struts about with other good works by which he praises himself and not God, and puts his trust in himself more than in God. Therefore he is justly rejected and the other chosen.

The reason of all this is that the higher and better the works are, the less show they make; and that everyone thinks they are easy, because it is evident that no one pretends to praise God's Name and honor so much as the very men who never do it and with their show of doing it, while the heart is without faith, cause the precious work to be despised. So that the Apostle St. Paul dare say boldly, Romans ii, that they blaspheme God's Name who make their boast of God's Law. For to name the Name of God and to write His honor on paper and on the walls is an easy matter; but genuinely to praise and bless Him in His good deeds and confidently to call upon Him in all adversities, these are truly the most rare, highest works, next to faith, so that if we were to see how few of them there are in Christendom, we might despair for very sorrow. And yet there is a constant increase of high, pretty, shining works of men's devising, or of works which look like these true works, but at bottom are all without faith and without faithfulness; in short, there is nothing good back of them. Thus also Isaiah 48 rebukes the people of Israel: "Hear ye this, ye which are called by the name of Israel, which swear by the Name of the Lord, and make mention of the God of Israel neither in truth, nor in righteousness"; that is, they did it not in the true faith and confidence, which is the real truth and righteousness, but trusted in themselves, their works and powers, and yet called upon God's Name and praised Him, two things which do not fit together.

21. The first work of this Commandment then is, to praise God in all His benefits, which are innumerable, so that such praise and thanksgiving ought also of right never to cease or end. For who can praise Him perfectly for the gift of natural life, not to mention all other temporal and eternal blessings? And so through this one part of the Commandment man is overwhelmed with good and precious works; if he do these in true faith, he has indeed not lived in vain. And in this matter none sin so much as the most resplendent saints, who are pleased with themselves and like to praise themselves or to hear themselves praised, honored and glorified before men.

Therefore the second work of this Commandment is, to be on one's guard, to flee from and to avoid all temporal honor and praise, and never to seek a name for oneself, or fame and a great reputation, that every one sing of him and tell of him; which is an exceedingly dangerous sin, and yet the most common of all, and, alas, little regarded. Everyone wants to be of importance and not to be the least, however small he may be; so deeply is nature sunk in the evil of its own conceit and in its self-confidence contrary to these two first Commandments.

Now the world regards this terrible vice as the highest virtue, and this makes it exceedingly dangerous for those who do not understand and have not had experience of God's Commandments and the histories of the Holy Scriptures, to read or hear the heathen books and histories. For all heathen books are poisoned through and through with this striving after praise and honor; in them men are taught by blind reason that they were not nor could be men of power and worth, who are not moved by praise and honor; but those are counted the best, who disregard body and life, friend and property and everything in the effort to win praise and honor. All the holy Fathers have complained of this vice and with one mind conclude that it is the very last vice to be overcome. St. Augustine says: "All other vices are practiced in evil works; only honor and self-satisfaction are practiced in and by means of good works."

Therefore if a man had nothing else to do except this second work of this Commandment, he would yet have to work all his life-time in order to fight this vice and drive it out, so common, so subtle, so quick and insidious is it. Now we all pass by this good work and exercise ourselves in many other lesser good works, nay, through other good works we overthrow this and forget it entirely. So the holy Name of God, which alone should be honored, is taken in vain and dishonored through our own cursed name, self-approval and honor-seeking. And this sin is more grievous before God than murder and adultery; but its wickedness is not so clearly seen as that of murder, because of its subtlety, for it is not accomplished in the coarse flesh, but in the spirit.

22. Some think it is good for young people that they be enticed by reputation and honor, and again by shame of and dishonor, and so be induced to do good. For there are many who do the good and leave the evil undone out of fear of shame and love of honor, and so do what they would otherwise by no means do or leave undone. These I leave to their opinion. But at present we are seeking how true good works are to be done, and they who are inclined to do them surely do not need to be driven by the fear of shame and the love of honor; they have, and are to have a higher and far nobler incentive, namely, God's commandment, God's fear, God's approval, and their faith and love toward God. They who have not, or regard not this motive, and let shame and honor drive them, these also have their reward, as the Lord says in Matthew chapter 6; and as the motive, so is also the work and the reward: none of them is good, except only in the eyes of the world.

Now I hold that a young person could be more easily trained and incited by God's fear and commandments than by any other means. Yet where these do not help, we must endure that they do the good and leave the evil for the sake of shame and of honor, just as we must also endure wicked men or the imperfect, of whom we spoke above; nor can we do more than tell them that their works are not satisfactory and right before God, and so leave them until they learn to do right for the sake of God's commandments also. Just as young children are induced to pray, fast, learn, etc., by gifts and promises of the parents, even though it would not be good to treat them so all their lives, so that they never learn to do good in the fear of God: far worse, if they become accustomed to do good for the sake of praise and honor.

23. But this is true, that we must none the less have a good name and honor, and every one ought so to live that nothing evil can be said of him, and that he give offence to no one, as St. Paul says in Romans chapter 12: "We are to be zealous to do good, not only before God, but also before all men." And in 2 Corinthians chapter 4: "We walk so honestly that no man knows anything against us." But there must be

great diligence and care, lest such honor and good name puff up the heart, and the heart find pleasure in them. Here the saying of Solomon holds: "As the fire in the furnace proveth the gold, so man is proved by the mouth of him that praises him." Few and most spiritual men must they be, who, when honored and praised, remain indifferent and unchanged, so that they do not care for it, nor feel pride and pleasure in it, but remain entirely free, ascribe all their honor and fame to God, offering it to Him alone, and using it only to the glory of God, to the edification of their neighbors, and in no way to their own benefit or advantage; so that a man trust not in his own honor, nor exalt himself above the most incapable, despised man on earth, but acknowledge himself a servant of God, Who has given him the honor in order that with it he may serve God and his neighbor, just as if He had commanded him to distribute some gulden to the poor for His sake. So He says in Matthew chapter 5: "Your light shall shine before men, so that they may see your good works and glorify your Father Who is in heaven." He does not say, "they shall praise you," but "your works shall only serve them to edification, that through them they may praise God in you and in themselves." This is the correct use of God's Name and honor, when God is thereby praised through the edification of others. And if men want to praise us and not God in us, we are not to endure it, but with all our powers forbid it and flee from it as from the most grievous sin and robbery of divine honor.

24. Hence it comes that God frequently permits a man to fall into or remain in grievous sin, in order that he may be put to shame in his own eyes and in the eyes of all men, who otherwise could not have kept himself from this great vice of vain honor and fame, if he had remained constant in his great gifts and virtues; so God must ward off this sin by means of other grievous sins, that His Name alone may be honored; and thus one sin becomes the other's medicine, because of our perverse wickedness, which not only does the evil, but also misuses all that is good.

Now see how much a man has to do, if he would do good works, which always are at hand in great number, and with which he is surrounded on all sides; but, alas! because of his blindness, he passes them by and seeks and runs after others of his own devising and pleasure, against which no man can sufficiently speak and no man can sufficiently guard. With this all the prophets had to contend, and for this reason they were all slain, only because they rejected such self-devised works and preached only God's commandments, as one of them says, Jeremiah vii: "Thus saith the God of Israel unto you: Take your burnt offerings unto all your sacrifices and eat your burnt-offerings and your flesh yourselves; for concerning these things I have commanded you nothing, but this thing commanded I you: Obey My voice (that is, not what seems right and good to you, but what I bid you), and walk in the way that I have commanded you." And Deuteronomy xii: "Thou shalt not do whatsoever is right in thine own eyes, but what thy God has commanded thee."

These and numberless like passages of Scripture are spoken to tear man not only from sins, but also from the works which seem to men to be good and right, and to turn men, with a single mind, to the simple meaning of God's commandment only, that they shall diligently observe this only and always, as it is written, Exodus 13: "These commandments shall be for a sign unto thee upon thine hand, and for a memorial between thine eyes." And Psalm 1: "A godly man meditates in God's Law day and night." For we have more than enough and too much to do, if we are to satisfy only God's commandments. He has given us such commandments that if we understand them aright, we dare not for a moment be idle, and might easily forget all other works. But the evil spirit, who never rests, when he cannot lead us to the left into evil works, fights on our right through self-devised works that seem good, but against which God has commanded in Deuteronomy 28 and Joshua 23, "Ye shall not go aside from My commandments to the right hand or to the left."

25. The third work of this Commandment is to call upon God's Name in every need. For this God regards as keeping His Name holy and greatly honoring it, if we name and call upon it in adversity and need. And this is really why He sends us so much trouble, suffering, adversity and even death, and lets us live in many wicked, sinful affections, that He may thereby urge man and give him much reason to run to Him, to cry aloud to Him, to call upon His holy Name, and thus to fulfill this work of the Second Commandment, as He says in Psalm 50:15: "Call upon Me in the day of trouble; I will deliver thee, and thou shalt glorify Me; for I desire the sacrifice of praise." And this is the way whereby thou canst come unto salvation; for through such works man perceives and learns what God's Name is, how powerful it is to help all who call upon it; and whereby confidence and faith grow mightily, and these are the fulfilling of the first and highest Commandment. This is the experience of David in Psalm 54: "Thou hast delivered me out of all trouble, therefore will I praise Thy Name and confess that it is lovely and sweet." And Psalm 91 says, "Because he hath set his hope upon Me, therefore will I deliver him: I will help him, because he hath known My Name."

Lo! What man is there on earth, who would not all his life long have enough to do with this work? For who lives an hour without trials? I will not mention the trials of adversity, which are innumerable. For this is the most dangerous trial of all, when there is no trial and everything is and goes well; for then a man is tempted to forget God, to become too bold and to misuse the times of prosperity. Yea, here he has ten times more need to call upon God's Name than when in adversity. Since it is written in Psalm 91, "A thousand shall fall on the left hand and ten thousand on the right hand."

So too we see in broad day, in all men's daily experience, that more heinous sins and vice occur when there is peace, when all things are cheap and there are good times, than when war, pestilence, sicknesses and all manner of misfortune burden us; so that Moses also fears for his people, lest they forsake God's commandment for no other reason than because they are too full, too well provided for and have too much peace, as he says, Deuteronomy chapter 32 "My people is waxed rich, full and fat; therefore has it forsaken its God." Wherefore also God let many of its enemies remain and would not drive them out, in order that they should not have peace and must exercise themselves in the keeping of God's commandments, as it is written in Judges chapter 3. So He deals with us also, when He sends us all kinds of misfortune: so exceedingly careful is He of us, that He may teach us and drive us to honor and call upon His Name, to gain confidence and faith toward Him, and so to fulfill the first two Commandments.

26. Here foolish men run into danger, and especially the work-righteous saints, and those who want to be more than others; they teach men to make the sign of the cross; one arms himself with letters, another runs to the fortunetellers; one seeks this, another that, if only they may thereby escape misfortune and be secure. It is beyond telling what a devilish allurement attaches to this trifling with sorcery, conjuring and superstition, all of which is done only that men may not need God's Name and put no trust in it. Here great dishonor is done the Name of God and the first two Commandments, in that men look to the devil, men or creatures for that which should be sought and found in God alone, through naught but a pure faith and confidence, and a cheerful meditation of and calling upon His holy Name.

Now examine this closely for yourself and see whether this is not a gross, mad perversion: the devil, men and creatures they must believe, and trust to them for the best; without such faith and confidence nothing holds or helps. How shall the good and faithful God reward us for not believing and trusting Him as much or more than man and the devil, although He not only promises help and sure assistance, but also commands us confidently to look for it, and gives and urges all manner of reasons why we should place such faith and confidence in Him? Is it not lamentable and pitiable that the devil or man, who commands nothing and does not urge, but only promises, is set above

God, Who promises, urges and commands; and that more is thought of them than of God Himself? We ought truly to be ashamed of ourselves and learn from the example of those who trust the devil or men. For if the devil, who is a wicked, lying spirit, keeps faith with all those who ally themselves with him, how much more will not the most gracious, all-truthful God keep faith, if a man trusts Him? Nay, is it not rather He alone Who will keep faith? A rich man trusts and relies upon his money and possessions, and they help him; and we are not willing to trust and rely upon the living God, that He is willing and able to help us? We say: Gold makes bold; and it is true, as it says, "Gold is a thing wherein men trust." But far greater is the courage which the highest eternal Good gives, wherein trust, not men, but only God's children.

27. Even if none of these adversities constrain us to call upon God's Name and to trust Him, yet were sin alone more than sufficient to train and to urge us on in this work. For sin has hemmed us in with three strong, mighty armies. The first is our own flesh, the second the world, the third the evil spirit, by which three we are without ceasing oppressed and troubled; whereby God gives us occasion to do good works without ceasing, namely, to fight with these enemies and sins. The flesh seeks pleasure and peace, the world seeks riches, favor, power and honor, the evil spirit seeks pride, glory, that a man be well thought of, and other men be despised.

And these three are all so powerful that each one of them is alone sufficient to fight a man, and yet there is no way we can overcome them, except only by calling upon the holy Name of God in a firm faith, as Solomon says, Proverbs 18: "The Name of the Lord is a strong tower; the righteous runneth into it, and is set aloft." And David, in Psalm 116: "I will drink the cup of salvation, and call upon the Name of the Lord." Again, in Psalm 18: "I will call upon the Lord with praise: so shall I be saved from all mine enemies." These works and the power of God's Name have become unknown to us, because we are not accustomed to it, and have never seriously fought with sins, and have not needed His Name, because we are trained only in our self devised works, which we were able to do with our own powers.

28. Further works of this Commandment are: that we shall not swear, curse, lie, deceive and conjure with the holy Name of God, and otherwise misuse it; which are very simple matters and well known to everyone, being the sins which have been almost exclusively preached and proclaimed under this Commandment. These also include, that we shall prevent others from making sinful use of God's Name by lying, swearing, deceiving, cursing, conjuring, and otherwise. Herein again much occasion is given for doing good and warding off evil.

But the greatest and most difficult work of this Commandment is to protect the holy Name of God against all who misuse it in a spiritual manner, and to proclaim it to all men. For it is not enough that I, for myself and in myself, praise and call upon God's Name in prosperity and adversity. I must step forth and for the sake of God's honor and Name bring upon myself the enmity of all men, as Christ said to His disciples: "Ye shall be hated of all men for My Name's sake." Here we must provoke to anger father, mother, and the best of friends. Here we must strive against spiritual and temporal powers, and be accused of disobedience. Here we must stir up against us the rich, learned, holy, and all that is of repute in the world. And although this is especially the duty of those who are commanded to preach God's Word, yet every Christian is also obligated to do so when time and place demand. For we must for the holy Name of God risk and give up all that we have and can do, and show by our deeds that we love God and His Name, His honor and His praise above all things, and trust Him above all things, and expect good from Him; thereby confessing that we regard Him as the highest good, for the sake of which we let go and give up all other goods.

29. Here we must first of all resist all wrong, where truth or righteousness suffers violence or need, and dare make no distinction of persons, as some do, who fight most actively and busily against the wrong which is done to the rich, the powerful, and their own friends; but when it is done to the poor, or the despised or their own enemy, they are quiet and patient. These see the Name and the honor of God not as it is, but through a painted glass, and measure truth or righteousness according to the persons, and do not consider their deceiving eye, which looks more on the person than on the thing. These are hypocrites within and have only the appearance of defending the truth. For they well know that there is no danger when one helps the rich, the powerful, the learned and one's own friends, and can in turn enjoy their protection and be honored by them.

Thus it is very easy to fight against the wrong which is done to popes, kings, princes, bishops and other big-wigs. Here each wants to be the most pious, where there is no great need. O how sly is here the deceitful Adam with his demand; how finely does he cover his greed of profit with the name of truth and righteousness and God's honor! But when something happens to a poor and insignificant man, there the deceitful eye does not find much profit, but cannot help seeing the disfavor of the powerful; therefore he lets the poor man remain unhelped. And who could tell the extent of this vice in Christendom? God says in Psalm 82, "How long will ye judge unjustly, and accept the persons of the wicked? Judge the matter of the poor and fatherless, demand justice for the poor and needy; deliver the poor and rid the forsaken out of the hand of the wicked." But it is not done, and therefore the text continues: "They know not, neither will they understand; they walk on in darkness"; that is, the truth they do not see, but they stop at the reputation of the great, however unrighteous they are; and do not consider the poor, however righteous they are.

30. See, here would be many good works. For the greater portion of the powerful, rich and friends do injustice and oppress the poor, the lowly, and their own opponents; and the greater the men, the worse the deeds; and where we cannot by force prevent it and help the truth, we should at least confess it, and do what we can with words, not take the part of the unrighteous, not approve them, but speak the truth boldly.

What would it help a man if he did all manner of good, made pilgrimages to Rome and to all holy places, acquired all indulgences, built all churches and endowed houses, if he were found guilty of sin against the Name and honor of God, not speaking of them and neglecting them, and regarding his possessions, honor, favor and friends more than the truth (which is God's Name and honor)? Or who is he, before whose door and into whose house such good works do not daily come, so that he would have no need to travel far or to ask after good works? And if we consider the life of men, how in every place men act so very rashly and lightly in this respect, we must cry out with the prophet, *Omnis homo mendax,* "All men are liars, lie and deceive"; for the real good works they neglect, and adorn and paint themselves with the most insignificant, and want to be pious, to mount to heaven in peaceful security.

But if you should say: "Why does not God do it alone and Himself, since He can and knows how to help each one?" Yes, He can do it; but He does not want to do it alone; He wants us to work with Him, and does us the honor to want to work His work with us and through us. And if we are not willing to accept such honor, He will, after all, perform the work alone, and help the poor; and those who were unwilling to help Him and have despised the great honor of doing His work, He will condemn with the unrighteous, because they have made common cause with the unrighteous. Just as He alone is blessed, but He wants to do us the honor and not be alone in His blessedness, but have us to be blessed with Him. And if He were to do it alone, His Commandments would be given us in vain, because no one would have occasion to exercise himself in the great works of these Commandments, and no one would test himself to see whether he regards God and His Name as the highest good, and for His sake risks everything.

31. It also belongs to this work to resist all false, seductive, erroneous, heretical doctrines, every misuse of spiritual power. Now this is much higher, for these use the holy Name of God itself to fight against the Name of God. For this reason it seems a great thing and a dangerous to resist them, because they assert that he who resists them resists God and all His saints, in whose place they sit and whose power they use, saying that Christ said of them, "He that heareth you, heareth Me, and he that despiseth you, despiseth Me." On which words they lean heavily, become insolent and bold to say, to do, and to leave undone what they please; put to the ban, accurse, rob, murder, and practice all their wickedness, in whatever way they please and can invent, without any hindrance.

Now Christ did not mean that we should listen to them in everything they might say and do, but only then when they present to us His Word, the Gospel, not their word, His work, and not their work. How else could we know whether their lies and sins were to be avoided? There must be some rule, to what extent we are to hear and to follow them, and this rule cannot be given by them, but must be established by God over them, that it may serve us as a guide, as we shall hear in the Fourth Commandment.

It must be, indeed, that even in the spiritual estate the greater part preach false doctrine and misuse spiritual power, so that thus occasion may be given us to do the works of this Commandment, and that we be tried, to see what we are willing to do and to leave undone against such blasphemers for the sake of God's honor.

Oh, if we were God-fearing in this matter, how often would the knaves of officials have to decree their papal and episcopal ban in vain! How weak the Roman thunderbolts would become! How often would many a one have to hold his tongue, to whom the world must now give ear! How few preachers would be found in Christendom! But it has gotten the upper hand: whatever they assert and in whatever way, that must be right. Here no one fights for God's Name and honor, and I hold that no greater or more frequent sin is done in external works than under this head. It is a matter so high that few understand it, and, besides, adorned with God's Name and power, dangerous to touch. But the prophets of old were masters in this; also the apostles, especially St. Paul, who did not allow it to trouble them whether the highest or the lowest priest had said it, or had done it in God's Name or in his own. They looked on the works and words, and held them up to God's Commandment, no matter whether big John or little Nick said it, or whether they had done it in God's Name or in man's. And for this they had to die, and of such dying there would be much more to say in our time, for things are much worse now. But Christ and St. Peter and Paul must cover all this with their holy names, so that no more infamous cover for infamy has been found on earth than the most holy and most blessed Name of Jesus Christ!

One might shudder to be alive, simply because of the misuse and blasphemy of the holy Name of God; through which, if it shall last much longer, we will, as I fear, openly worship the devil as a god; so completely do the spiritual authorities and the learned lack all understanding in these things. It is high time that we pray God earnestly that He hallow His Name. But it will cost blood, and they who enjoy the inheritance of the holy martyrs and are won with their blood, must again make martyrs. Of this, more another time.

Thou Shalt Hallow the Day of Rest: The Third (Fourth) Commandment

1. We have now seen how many good works there are in the Second Commandment, which however are not good in themselves, unless they are done in faith and in the assurance of divine favor; and how much we must do, if we take heed to this Commandment alone, and how we, alas! busy ourselves much with other works, which have no agreement at all with it. Now follows the Third Commandment: "Thou shalt hallow the day of rest." In the First Commandment is prescribed our heart's attitude toward God in thoughts, in the Second, that of our mouth in words, in this Third is prescribed our attitude toward God in works; and it is the first and right table of Moses, on which these three Commandments are written, and they govern man on the right side, namely, in the things which concern God, and in which God has to do with man and man with God, without the mediation of any creature.

The first works of this Commandment are plain and outward, which we commonly call worship, such as going to mass, praying, and hearing a sermon on holy days. So understood there are very few works in this Commandment; and these, if they are not done in assurance of and with faith in God's favor, are nothing, as was said above. Hence it would also be a good thing if there were fewer saint's days, since in our times the works done on them are for the greater part worse than those of the work days, what with loafing, gluttony, and drunkenness, gambling and other evil deeds; and then, the mass and the sermon are listened to without edification, the prayer is spoken without faith. It almost happens that men think it is sufficient that we look on at the mass with our eyes, hear the preaching with our ears, and say the prayers with our mouths. It is all so formal and superficial! We do not think that we might receive something out of the mass into our hearts, learn and remember something out of the preaching, seek, desire and expect something in our prayer. Although in this matter the bishops and priests, or they to whom the work of preaching is entrusted, are most at fault, because they do not preach the Gospel, and do not teach the people how they ought to look on at mass, hear preaching and pray. Therefore, we will briefly explain these three works.

2. In the mass it is necessary that we attend with our a hearts also; and we do attend, when we exercise faith in our hearts. Here we must repeat the words of Christ, when He institutes the mass and says, "Take and eat, this is My Body, which is given for you"; in like manner over the cup, "Take and drink ye all of it: this is a new, everlasting Testament in My Blood, which is shed for you and for many for the remission of sins. This shall ye do, as oft as ye do it, in remembrance of Me." In these words Christ has made for Himself a memorial or anniversary, to be daily observed in all Christendom, and has added to it a glorious, rich, great testament, in which no interest, money or temporal possessions are bequeathed and distributed, but the forgiveness of all sins, grace and mercy unto eternal life, that all who come to this memorial shall have the same testament; and then He died, whereby this testament has become permanent and irrevocable. In proof and evidence of which, instead of letter and seal, He has left with us His own Body and Blood under the bread and wine.

Here there is need that a man practice the first works of this Commandment right well, that he doubt not that what Christ has said is true, and consider the testament sure, so that he make not Christ a liar. For if you are present at mass and do not consider nor believe that here Christ through His testament has bequeathed and given you forgiveness of all your sins, what else is it, than as if you said: "I do not know or do not believe that it is true that forgiveness of my sins is here bequeathed and given me"? Oh, how many masses there are in the world at present! but how few who hear them with such faith and benefit! Most grievously is God provoked to anger thereby. For this reason also no one shall or can reap any benefit from the mass except he be in trouble of soul and long for divine mercy, and desire to be rid of his sins; or, if he have an evil intention, he must be changed during the mass, and come to have a desire for this testament. For this reason in olden times no open sinner was allowed to be present at the mass.

When this faith is rightly present, the heart must be made joyful by the testament, and grow warm and melt in God's love. Then will follow praise and thanksgiving with a pure heart, from which the mass is called in Greek *Eucharistia*, that is, "thanksgiving," because we praise and thank God for this comforting, rich, blessed testament, just as he gives thanks, praises and is joyful, to whom a good friend has presented a thousand and more gulden. Although Christ often fares like those who make several persons rich by their testament, and these persons never think of them, nor praise or thank them. So our masses at present are merely celebrated, without our knowing why or wherefore, and consequently we neither give thanks nor love nor praise, remain parched and hard, and have enough with our little prayer. Of this, more another time.

3. The sermon ought to be nothing else than the proclamation of this testament. But who can hear it if no one preaches it? Now, they who ought to preach it, themselves do not know it. This is why the sermons ramble off into other unprofitable stories, and thus Christ is forgotten, while we fare like the man in 2 Kings chapter 7: we see our riches but do not enjoy them. Of which the Preacher also says, "This is a great evil, when God giveth a man riches, and giveth him not power to enjoy them." So we look on at unnumbered masses and do not know whether the mass be a testament, or what it be, just as if it were any other common good work by itself. O God, how exceeding blind we are! But where this is rightly preached, it is necessary that it be diligently heard, grasped, retained, often thought of, and that the faith be thus strengthened against all the temptation of sin, whether past, or present, or to come.

Lo! This is the only ceremony or practice which Christ has instituted, in which His Christians shall assemble, exercise themselves and keep it with one accord; and this He did not make to be a mere work like other ceremonies, but placed into it a rich, exceeding great treasure, to be offered and bestowed upon all who believe on it.

This preaching should induce sinners to grieve over their sins, and should kindle in them a longing for the treasure. It must, therefore, be a grievous sin not to hear the Gospel, and to despise such a treasure and so rich a feast to which we are bidden; but a much greater sin not to preach the Gospel, and to let so many people who would gladly hear it perish, since Christ has so strictly commanded that the Gospel and this testament be preached, that He does not wish even the mass to be celebrated, unless the Gospel be preached, as He says: "As oft as ye do this, remember me"; that is, as St. Paul says, "Ye shall preach of His death." For this reason it is dreadful and horrible in our times to be a bishop, pastor and preacher; for no one any longer knows this testament, to say nothing of their preaching it, although this is their highest and only duty and obligation. How heavily must they give account for so many souls who must perish because of this lack in preaching.

4. We should pray, not as the custom is, counting many pages or beads, but fixing our mind upon some pressing need, desire it with all earnestness, and exercise faith and confidence toward God in the matter, in such wise that we do not doubt that we shall be heard. So St. Bernard instructs his brethren and says: "Dear brethren, you shall by no means despise your prayer, as if it were in vain, for I tell you of a truth that, before you have uttered the words, the prayer is already recorded in heaven; and you shall confidently expect from God one of two things: either that your prayer will be granted, or that, if it will not be granted, the granting of it would not be good for you."

Prayer is, therefore, a special exercise of faith, and faith makes the prayer so acceptable that either it will surely be granted, or something better than we ask will be given in its stead. So also says St. James: "Let him who asketh of God not waver in faith; for if he wavers, let not that man think that he shall receive any thing of the Lord." This is a clear statement, which says directly: he who does not trust, receives nothing, neither that which he asks, nor anything better.

And to call forth such faith, Christ Himself has said in Mark chapter 11 "Therefore I say unto you, What things soever ye desire, when ye pray, believe that ye receive them, and ye shall surely have them." And in Luke chapter 11: "Ask, and it shall be given you; seek, and ye shall find; knock, and it shall be opened unto you; for every one that asketh receiveth; and he that seeketh findeth; and to him that knocketh it shall be opened. Or what father is there of you, who, if his son shall ask bread, will he give him a stone? or if he ask a fish, will he give him a serpent? or if he ask an egg, will he give him a scorpion? But if you know how to give good gifts to your children, and you yourselves are not naturally good, how much more shall your Father which is in heaven give a good spirit to all them that ask Him!"

5. Who is so hard and stone-like, that such mighty words ought not to move him to pray with all confidence! joyfully and gladly? But how many prayers must be reformed, if we are to pray aright according to these words! Now, indeed, all churches and monastic houses are full of praying and singing, but how does it happen that so little improvement and benefit result from it, and things daily grow worse? The reason is none other than that which St. James indicates when he says: "You ask much and receive not, because ye ask amiss." For where this faith and confidence is not in the prayer, the prayer is dead, and nothing more than a grievous labor and work. If anything is given for it, it is none the less only temporal benefit without any blessing and help for the soul; nay, to the great injury and blinding of souls, so that they go their way, babbling much with their mouths, regardless of whether they receive, or desire, or trust; and in this unbelief, the

state of mind most opposed to the exercise of faith and to the nature of prayer, they remain hardened.

From this it follows that one who prays aright never doubts that his prayer is surely acceptable and heard, although the very thing for which he prays be not given him. For we are to lay our need before God in prayer, but not prescribe to Him a measure, manner, time or place; but if He wills to give it to us better or in another way than we think, we are to leave it to Him; for frequently we do not know what we pray, as St. Paul says in Romans chapter 8; and God works and gives above all that we understand, as he says in Ephesians chapter 3, so that there be no doubt that the prayer is acceptable and heard, and we yet leave to God the time, place, measure and limit; He will surely do what is right. They are the true worshipers, who worship God in spirit and in truth. For they who believe not that they will be heard, sin upon the left hand against this Commandment, and go far astray with their unbelief. But they who set a limit for Him, sin upon the other side, and come too close with their tempting of God. So He has forbidden both, that we should err from His Commandment neither to the left nor to the right, that is, neither with unbelief nor with tempting, but with simple faith remain on the straight road, trusting Him, and yet setting Him no bounds.

6. Thus we see that this Commandment, like the Second, is to be nothing else than a doing and keeping of the First Commandment, that is, of faith, trust, confidence, hope and love to God, so that in all the Commandments the First may be the captain, and faith the chief work and the life of all other works, without which, as was said, they cannot be good.

But if you say: "What if I cannot believe that my prayer is heard and accepted?" I answer: For this very reason faith, prayer and all other good works are commanded, that you shall know what you can and what you cannot do. And when you find that you cannot so believe and do, then you are humbly to confess it to God, and so begin with a weak spark of faith and daily strengthen it more and more by exercising it in all your living and doing. For as touching infirmity of faith (that is, of the First and highest Commandment), there is no one on earth who does not have his good share of it. For even the holy Apostles in the Gospel, and especially St. Peter, were weak in faith, so that they also prayed Christ and said: "Lord, increase our faith "; and He very frequently rebukes them because they have so little faith.

Therefore you shall not despair, nor give up, even if you find that you do not believe as firmly as you ought and wish, in your prayer or in other works. Nay, you shall thank God with all your heart that He thus reveals to you your weakness, through which He daily teaches and admonishes you how much you need to exercise yourself and daily strengthen yourself in faith. For how many do you see who habitually pray, sing, read, work and seem to be great saints, and yet never get so far as to know where they stand in respect of the chief work, faith; and so in their blindness they lead astray themselves and others; think they are very well off, and so unknowingly build on the sand of their works without any faith, not on God's mercy and promise through a firm, pure faith.

Therefore, however long we live, we shall always have our hands full to remain, with all our works and sufferings, pupils of the First Commandment and of faith, and not to cease to learn. No one knows what a great thing it is to trust God alone, except he who attempts it with his works.

7. Again: if no other work were commanded, would not prayer alone suffice to exercise the whole life of man in faith? For this work the spiritual estate has been specially established, as indeed in olden times some Fathers prayed day and night. Nay, there is no Christian who does not have time to pray without ceasing. But I mean the spiritual praying, that is: no one is so heavily burdened with his labor, but that if he will he can, while working, speak with God in his heart,

lay before Him his need and that of other men, ask for help, make petition, and in all this exercise and strengthen his faith.

This is what the Lord means in Luke 18, when He says, "Men ought always to pray, and never cease," although in Matthew chapter 6 He forbids the use of much speaking and long prayers, because of which He rebukes the hypocrites; not because the lengthy prayer of the lips is evil, but because it is not that true prayer which can be made at all times, and without the inner prayer of faith is nothing. For we must also practice the outward prayer in its proper time, especially in the mass, as this Commandment requires, and wherever it is helpful to the inner prayer and faith, whether in the house or in the field, in this work or in that; of which we have no time now to speak more. For this belongs to the Lord's Prayer, in which all petitions and spoken prayer are summed up in brief words.

8. Where now are they who desire to know and to do good works? Let them undertake prayer alone, and rightly exercise themselves in faith, and they will find that it is true, as the holy Fathers have said, that there is no work like prayer. Mumbling with the mouth is easy, or at least considered easy, but with earnestness of heart to follow the words in deep devotion, that is, with desire and faith, so that one earnestly desires what the words say, and not to doubt that it will be heard: that is a great deed in God's eyes.

Here the evil spirit hinders men with all his powers. Oh, how often will he here prevent the desire to pray, not allow us to find time and place, nay, often also raise doubts, whether a man is worthy to ask anything of such a Majesty as God is, and so confuse us that a man himself does not know whether it is really true that he prays or not; whether it is possible that his prayer is acceptable, and other such strange thoughts. For the evil spirit knows well how powerful one man's truly believing prayer is, and how it hurts him, and how it benefits all men. Therefore he does not willingly let it happen.

When so tempted, a man must indeed be wise, and not doubt that he and his prayer are, indeed, unworthy before such infinite Majesty; in no wise dare he trust his worthiness, or because of his unworthiness grow faint; but he must heed God's command and cast this up to Him, and hold it before the devil, and say: "Because of my worthiness I do nothing, because of my unworthiness I cease from nothing. I pray and work only because God of His pure mercy has promised to hear and to be gracious to all unworthy men, and not only promised it, but He has also most sternly, on pain of His everlasting displeasure and wrath, commanded us to pray, to trust and to receive. If it has not been too much for that high Majesty so solemnly and highly to obligate His unworthy worms to pray, to trust, and to receive from Him, how shall it be too much for me to take such command upon myself with all joy, however worthy or unworthy I may be?" Thus we must drive out the devil's suggestion with God's command. Thus will he cease, and in no other way whatever.

9. But what are the things which we must bring before Almighty God in prayer and lamentation, to exercise faith thereby? Answer: First, every man's own besetting need and trouble, of which David says, Psalm 32 "Thou art my refuge in all trouble which compasseth me about; Thou art my comfort, to preserve me from all evil which surrounds me." Likewise, Psalm 142 "I cried unto the Lord with my voice; with my voice unto the Lord did I make my supplication. I poured out my complaint before Him; I showed before Him my trouble." In the mass a Christian shall keep in mind the short-comings or excesses he feels, and pour out all these freely before God with weeping and groaning, as woefully as he can, as to his faithful Father, who is ready to help him. And if you do not know or recognize your need, or have no trouble, then you shall know that you are in the worst possible plight. For this is the greatest trouble, that you find yourself so hardened, hard-hearted and insensible that no trouble moves you.

There is no better mirror in which to see your need than simply the Ten Commandments, in which you will find what you lack and what you should seek. If, therefore, you find in yourself a weak faith, small hope and little love toward God; and that you do not praise and honor God, but love your own honor and fame, think much of the favor of men, do not gladly hear mass and sermon, are indolent in prayer, in which things everyone has faults, then you shall think more of these faults than of all bodily harm to goods, honor and life, and believe that they are worse than death and all mortal sickness. These you shall earnestly lay before God, lament and ask for help, and with all confidence expect help, and believe that you are heard and shall obtain help and mercy.

Then go forward into the Second Table of the Commandments, and see how disobedient you have been and still are toward father and mother and all in authority; how you sin against your neighbor with anger, hatred and evil words; how you are tempted to unchastity, covetousness and injustice in word and deed against your neighbor; and you will doubtless find that you are full of all need and misery, and have reason enough to weep even drops of blood, if you could.

10. But I know well that many are so foolish as not to want to ask for such things, unless they first be conscious that they are pure, and believe that God hears no one who is a sinner. All this is the work of those false preachers, who teach men to begin, not with faith and trust in God's favor, but with their own works.

Look you, wretched man! if you have broken a leg, or the peril of death overtakes you, you call upon God, this Saint and that, and do not wait until your leg is healed, or the danger is past: you are not so foolish as to think that God hears no one whose leg is broken, or who is in bodily danger. Nay, you believe that God shall hear most of all when you are in the greatest need and fear. Why, then, are you so foolish here, where there is immeasurably greater need and eternal hurt, and do not want to ask for faith, hope, love, humility, obedience, chastity, gentleness, peace, righteousness, unless you are already free of all your unbelief, doubt, pride, disobedience, unchastity, anger, covetousness and unrighteousness. Although the more you find yourself lacking in these things, the more and more diligently you ought to pray or cry.

So blind are we: with our bodily sickness and need we run to God; with the soul's sickness we run from Him, and are unwilling to come back before we are well, exactly as if there could be one God who could help the body, and another God who could help the soul; or as if we would help ourselves in spiritual need, although it really is greater than the bodily need. Such plan and counsel is of the devil.

Not so, my good man! If you wish to be cured of sin, you must not withdraw from God, but run to Him, and pray with much more confidence than if a bodily need had overtaken you. God is not hostile to sinners, but only to unbelievers, that is, to such as do not recognize and lament their sin, nor seek help against it from God, but in their own presumption wish first to purify themselves, are unwilling to be in need of His grace, and will not suffer Him to be a God Who gives to everyone and takes nothing in return.

11. All this has been said of prayer for personal needs, and of prayer in general. But the prayer which really belongs to this Commandment and is called a work of the Holy Day, is far better and greater, and is to be made for all Christendom, for all the need of all men, of foe and friend, especially for those who belong to the parish or bishopric. Thus St. Paul commanded his disciple Timothy: "exhort thee, that thou see to it, that prayers and intercessions be made for all men, for kings, and for all that are in authority, that we may lead a quiet and peaceable life in all godliness and honesty. For this is good and acceptable in the sight of God our Savior." For this reason Jeremiah, chapter 29, commanded the people of Israel to pray for the city and land of Babylon, because in the peace thereof they should have peace.

And Baruch 1: "Pray for the life of the king of Babylon and for the life of his son, that we may live in peace under their rule."

This common prayer is precious and the most powerful, and it is for its sake that we come together. For this reason also the Church is called a House of Prayer, because in it we are as a congregation with one accord to consider our need and the needs of all men, present them before God, and call upon Him for mercy. But this must be done with heart-felt emotion and sincerity, so that we feel in our hearts the need of all men, and that we pray with true sympathy for them, in true faith and confidence. Where such prayers are not made in the mass, it were better to omit the mass. For what sense is there in our coming together into a House of Prayer, which coming together shows that we should make common prayer and petition for the entire congregation, if we scatter these prayers, and so distribute them that everyone prays only for himself, and no one has regard for the other, nor concerns himself for another's need? How can that prayer be of help, good, acceptable and a common prayer, or a work of the Holy Day and of the assembled congregation, which they make who make their own petty prayers, one for this, the other for that, and have nothing but self-seeking, selfish prayers, which God hates?

12. A suggestion of this common prayer has been retained from ancient practice, when at the end of the sermon the Confession of Sins is said and prayer is made on the pulpit for all Christendom. But this should not be the end of the matter, as is now the custom and fashion; it should be an exhortation to pray throughout the entire mass for such need as the preacher makes us feel; and in order that we may pray worthily, he first exhorts us because of our sin, and thereby makes us humble. This should be done as briefly as possible, that then the entire congregation may confess their own sin and pray for every one with earnestness and faith.

Oh, if God granted that any congregation at all heard mass and prayed in this way, so that a common earnest heart-cry of the entire people would rise up to God, what immeasurable virtue and help would result from such a prayer! What more terrible thing could happen to all the evil spirits? What greater work could be done on earth, whereby so many pious souls would be preserved, so many sinners converted?

For, indeed, the Christian Church on earth has no greater power or work than such common prayer against everything that may oppose it. This the evil spirit knows well, and therefore he does all that he can to prevent such prayer. Gleefully he lets us go on building churches, endowing many monastic houses, making music, reading, singing, observing many masses, and multiplying ceremonies beyond all measure. This does not grieve him, nay, he helps us do it, that we may consider such things the very best, and think that thereby we have done our whole duty. But in that meanwhile this common, effectual and fruitful prayer perishes and its omission is unnoticed because of such display, in this he has what he seeks. For when prayer languishes, no one will take anything from him, and no one will withstand him. But if he noticed that we wished to practice this prayer, even if it were under a straw roof or in a pig-sty, he would indeed not endure it, but would fear such a pig-sty far more than all the high, big and beautiful churches, towers and bells in existence, if such prayer be not in them. It is indeed not a question of the places and buildings in which we assemble, but only of this unconquerable prayer, that we pray it and bring it before God as a truly common prayer.

13. The power of this prayer we see in the fact that in olden times Abraham prayed for the five cities, Sodom, Gomorrah, etc., Genesis 18, and accomplished so much, that if there had been ten righteous people in them, two in each city, God would not have destroyed them. What then could many men do, if they united in calling upon God earnestly and with sincere confidence?

St. James also says: "Dear brethren, pray for one another, that ye may be saved. For the prayer of a righteous man availeth much, a prayer that perseveres and does not cease" (that is, which does not cease asking ever more and more, although what it asks is not immediately granted, as some timid men do). And as an example in this matter he sets before us Elijah, the Prophet, "who was a man," he says, "as we are, and prayed, that it might not rain; and it rained not by the space of three years and six months. And he prayed again, and it rained, and everything became fruitful." There are many texts and examples in the Scriptures which urge us to pray, only that it be done with earnestness and faith. As David says, "The eyes of the Lord are upon the righteous, and His ears are open unto their cry." Again, "The Lord is nigh unto all them that call upon Him, to all that call upon Him in truth." Why does he add, "call upon Him in truth"? Because that is not prayer nor calling upon God when the mouth alone mumbles.

What should God do, if you come along with your mouth, book or Paternoster, and think of nothing except that you may finish the words and complete the number? So that if someone were to ask you what it all was about, or what it was that you prayed for, you yourself would not know; for you had not thought of laying this or that matter before God or desiring it. Your only reason for praying is that you are commanded to pray this and so much, and this you intend to do in full. What wonder that thunder and lightning frequently set churches on fire, because we thus make of the House of Prayer a house of mockery, and call that prayer in which we bring nothing before God and desire nothing from Him.

But we should do as they do who wish to ask a favor of great princes. These do not plan merely to babble a certain number of words, for the prince would think they mocked him, or were insane; but they put their request very plainly, and present their need earnestly, and then leave it to his mercy, in good confidence that he will grant it. So we must deal with God of definite things, namely, mention some present need, commend it to His mercy and good-will, and not doubt that it is heard; for He has promised to hear such prayer, which no earthly lord has done.

14. We are masters in this form of prayer when we suffer bodily need; when we are sick we call here upon St. Christopher, there upon St. Barbara; we vow a pilgrimage to St. James, to this place and to that; then we make earnest prayer, have a good confidence and every good kind of prayer. But when we are in our churches during mass, we stand like images of saints; know nothing to speak of or to lament; the beads rattle, the pages rustle and the mouth babbles; and that is all there is to it.

But if you ask what you shall speak of and lament in your prayer, you can easily learn from the Ten Commandments and the Lord's Prayer. Open your eyes and look into your life and the life of all Christians, especially of the spiritual estate, and you will find how faith, hope, love, obedience, chastity and every virtue languish, and all manner of heinous vices reign; what a lack there is of good preachers and prelates; how only knaves, children, fools and women rule. Then you will see that there were need every hour without ceasing to pray everywhere with tears of blood to God, Who is so terribly angry with men. And it is true that it has never been more necessary to pray than at this time, and it will be more so from now on to the end of the world. If such terrible crimes do not move you to lament and complain, do not permit yourself to be led astray by your rank, station, good works or prayer: there is no Christian vein or trait in you, however righteous you may be. But it has all been foretold, that when God's anger is greatest and Christendom suffers the greatest need, then petitioners and supplicants before God shall not be found, as Isaiah says with tears, chapter 64: "Thou art angry with us, and there is none that calleth upon Thy Name, that stirreth up himself to take hold of Thee." Likewise, Ezekiel 22: "I sought for a man among them, that should make up the hedge, and stand in the gap before me for the land, that I should not destroy it; but I found none. Therefore have I poured out Mine indignation upon them; I have consumed them with the fire of My wrath." With these words God indicates how He wants us to withstand Him and turn away His anger from one another, as it is frequently written of the Prophet Moses, that he restrained God, lest His anger should overwhelm the people of Israel.

15. But what will they do, who not only do not regard such misfortune of Christendom, and do not pray against it, but laugh at it, take pleasure in it, condemn, malign, sing and talk of their neighbor's sins, and yet dare, unafraid and unashamed, go to church, hear mass, say prayers, and regard themselves and are regarded as pious Christians? These truly are in need that we pray twice for them, if we pray once for those whom they condemn, talk about and laugh at. That there would be such is also prophesied by the thief on Christ's left hand, who blasphemed Him in His suffering, weakness and need; also by all those who reviled Christ on the Cross, when they should most of all have helped Him.

O God, how blind, nay, how insane have we Christians become! When will there be an end of wrath, O heavenly Father? That we mock at the misfortune of Christendom, to pray for which we gather together in Church and at the mass, that we blaspheme and condemn men, this is the fruit of our mad materialism. If the Turk destroys cities, country and people, and ruins churches, we think a great injury has been done Christendom. Then we complain, and urge kings and princes to war. But when faith perishes, love grows cold, God's Word is neglected, and all manner of sin flourishes, then no one thinks of fighting, nay, pope, bishops, priests and clergy, who ought to be generals, captains and standard-bearers in this spiritual warfare against these spiritual and many times worse Turks, these are themselves the very princes and leaders of such Turks and of the devil host, just as Judas was the leader of the Jews when they took Christ. It had to be an apostle, a bishop, a priest, one of the number of the best, who began the work of slaying Christ. So also must Christendom be laid waste by no others than those who ought to protect it, and yet are so insane that they are ready to eat up the Turks and at home themselves set house and sheep-cote on fire and let them burn up with the sheep and all other contents, and none the less worry about the wolf in the woods. Such are our times, and this is the reward we have earned by our ingratitude toward the endless grace which Christ has won for us freely with His precious blood, grievous labor and bitter death.

16. Lo! where are the idle ones, who do not know how to do good works? Where are they who run to Rome, to St. James, hither and thither? Take up this one single work of the mass, look on your neighbor's sin and ruin, and have pity on him; let it grieve you, tell it to God, and pray over it. Do the same for every other need of Christendom, especially of the rulers, whom God, for the intolerable punishment and torment of us all, allows to fall and be misled so terribly. If you do this diligently, be assured you are one of the best fighters and captains, not only against the Turks, but also against the devils and the powers of hell. But if you do it not, what would it help you though you performed all the miracles of the saints, and murdered all the Turks, and yet were found guilty of having disregarded your neighbor's need and of having thereby sinned against love? For Christ at the last day will not ask how much you have prayed, fasted, pilgrimaged, done this or that for yourself, but how much good you have done to others, even the very least.

Now without doubt among the "least" are also those who are in sin and spiritual poverty, captivity and need, of whom there are at present far more than of those who suffer bodily need. Therefore take heed: our own self-assumed good works lead us to and into ourselves, that we seek only our own benefit and salvation; but God's commandments drive us to our neighbor, that we may thereby benefit others to their salvation. Just as Christ on the Cross prayed not for Himself alone, but rather for us, when He said, "Father, forgive them, fort they know not what they do," so we also must pray for one another. From which every man may know that the slanderers, frivolous judges and despisers of other people are a perverted, evil race, who do nothing else than heap abuse on those for whom they ought to pray; in which vice no one is sunk so deep as those very men who do many good works of their own, and seem to men to be something extraordinary, and are honored because of their beautiful, splendid life in manifold good works.

17. Spiritually understood, this Commandment has a yet far higher work, which embraces the whole nature of man. Here it must be known that in Hebrew "Sabbath" means "rest," because on the seventh day God rested and ceased from all His works, which He had made, Genesis 2. Therefore He commanded also that the seventh day should be kept holy and that we cease from our works which we do the other six days. This Sabbath has now for us been changed into the Sunday, and the other days are called work-days; the Sunday is called rest-day or holiday or holy day. And would to God that in Christendom there were no holiday except the Sunday; that the festivals of Our Lady and of the Saints were all transferred to Sunday; then would many evil vices be done away with through the labor of the work-days, and lands would not be so drained and impoverished. But now we are plagued with many holidays, to the destruction of souls, bodies and goods; of which matter much might be said.

This rest or ceasing from labors is of two kinds, bodily and spiritual. For this reason this Commandment is also to be understood in two ways.

The bodily rest is that of which we have spoken above, namely, that we omit our business and work, in order that we may gather in the church, see mass, hear God's Word and make common prayer. This rest is indeed bodily and in Christendom no longer commanded by God, as the Apostle says, Colossians 2, "Let no man obligate you to any holiday whatever"--for they were of old a figure, but now the truth has been fulfilled, so that all days are holy days, as Isaiah says, chapter 66, "One holy day shall follow the other"; on the other hand, all days are workdays. Yet it is a necessity and ordained by the Church for the sake of the imperfect laity and working people, that they also may be able to come to hear God's Word. For, as we see, the priests and clergy celebrate mass every day, pray at all hours and train themselves in God's Word by study, reading and hearing. For this reason also they are freed from work before others, supported by tithes and have holy-day every day, and every day do the works of the holy-day, and have no work-day, but for them one day is as the other. And if we were all perfect, and knew the Gospel, we might work every day if we wished, or rest if we could. For a day of rest is at present not necessary nor commanded except only for the teaching of God's Word and prayer.

The spiritual rest, which God particularly intends in this Commandment, is this: that we not only cease from our labor and trade, but much more, that we let God alone work in us and that we do nothing of our own with all our powers. But how is this done? In this way: Man, corrupted by sin, has much wicked love and inclination toward all sins, as the Scriptures say, Genesis 8, "Man's heart and senses incline always to the evil," that is, to pride, disobedience, anger, hatred, covetousness, unchastity, etc., and summa summarum, in all that he does and leaves undone, he seeks his own profit, will and honor rather than God's and his neighbor's. Therefore all his works, all his words, all his thoughts, all his life are evil and not godly.

Now if God is to work and to live in him, all this vice and wickedness must be choked and up-rooted, so that there may be rest and a cessation of all our works, thoughts and life, and that henceforth (as St. Paul says, Galatians 2) it may be no longer we who live, but Christ Who lives, works and speaks in us. This is not accomplished with comfortable, pleasant days, but here we must hurt our nature and let it be hurt. Here begins the strife between the spirit and the flesh; here the spirit resists anger, lust, pride, while the flesh wants to be in pleasure, honor and comfort. Of this St. Paul says, Galatians 5, "They that are our Lord Christ's have crucified the flesh with its affections and lusts." Then follow the good works,--fasting, watching, labor, of which some say and write so much, although they know neither the source nor the purpose of these good works. Therefore we will now also speak of them.

18. This rest, namely, that our work cease and God alone work in us, is accomplished in two ways. First, through our own effort, secondly, through the effort or urging of others.

Our own effort is to be so made and ordered that, in the first place, when we see our flesh, senses, will and thoughts tempting us, we resist them and do not heed them, as the Wise Man says: "Follow not thine own desires." And Moses, Deuteronomy 12 "Thou shalt not do what is right in thine own eyes."

Here a man must make daily use of those prayers which David prays: "Lord, lead me in Thy path, and let me not walk in my own ways," and many like prayers, which are all summed up in the prayer, "Thy kingdom come." For the desires are so many, so various, and besides at times so nimble, so subtle and specious, through the suggestions of the evil one, that it is not possible for a man to control himself in his own ways. He must let hands and feet go, commend himself to God's governance, and entrust nothing to his reason, as Jeremiah says, "O Lord, I know that the way of man is not in his own power." We see proof of this, when the children of Israel went out of Egypt through the Wilderness, where there was no way, no food, no drink, no help. Therefore God went before them, by day in a bright cloud, by night in a fiery pillar, fed them with manna from heaven, and kept their garments and shoes that they waxed not old, as we read in the Books of Moses. For this reason we pray: "Thy kingdom come, that Thou rule us, and not we ourselves," for there is nothing more perilous in us than our reason and will. And this is the first and highest work of God in us and the best training, that we cease from our works, that we let our reason and will be idle, that we rest and commend ourselves to God in all things, especially when they seem to be spiritual and good.

19. After this comes the discipline of the flesh, to kill its gross, evil lust, to give it rest and relief. This we must kill and quiet with fasting, watching and labor, and from this we learn how much and why we shall fast, watch and labor.

There are, alas, many blind men, who practice their castigation, whether it be fasting, watching or labor, only because they think these are good works, intending by them to gain much merit. Far blinder still are they who measure their fasting not only by the quantity or duration, as these do, but also by the nature of the food, thinking that it is of far greater worth if they do not eat meat, eggs or butter. Beyond these are those who fast according to the saints, and according to the days; one fasting on Wednesday, another on Saturday, another on St. Barbara's day, another on St. Sebastian's day, and so on. These all seek in their fasting nothing beyond the work itself: when they have performed that, they think they have done a good work. I will here say nothing of the fact that some fast in such a way that they none the less drink themselves full; some fast by eating fish and other foods so lavishly that they would come much nearer to fasting if they ate meat, eggs and butter, and by so doing would obtain far better results from their fasting. For such fasting is not fasting, but a mockery of fasting and of God.

Therefore I allow everyone to choose his day, food and quantity for fasting, as he will, on condition that he do not stop with that, but have regard to his flesh; let him put upon it fasting, watching and labor according to its lust and wantonness, and no more, although pope, Church, bishop, father-confessor or anyone else whosoever have commanded it. For no one should measure and regulate fasting, watching and labor according to the character or quantity of the food, or according to the days, but according to the withdrawal or approach of the lust and wantonness of the flesh, for the sake of which alone the fasting, watching and labor is ordained, that is, to kill and to subdue them. If it were not for this lust, eating were as meritorious as fasting, sleeping as watching, idleness as labor, and each were as good as the other without all distinction.

20. Now, if someone should find that more wantonness arose in his flesh from eating fish than from eating eggs and meat, let him eat meat and not fish. Again, if he find that his head becomes confused and crazed or his body and stomach injured through fasting, or that it is not needful to kill the wantonness of his flesh, he shall let fasting

alone entirely, and eat, sleep, be idle as is necessary for his health, regardless whether it be against the command of the Church, or the rules of monastic orders: for no commandment of the Church, no law of an order can make fasting, watching and labor of more value than it has in serving to repress or to kill the flesh and its lusts. Where men go beyond this, and the fasting, eating, sleeping, watching are practiced beyond the strength of the body, and more than is necessary to the killing of the lust, so that through it the natural strength is ruined and the head is racked; then let no one imagine that he has done good works, or excuse himself by citing the commandment of the Church or the law of his order. He will be regarded as a man who takes no care of himself, and, as far as in him lies, has become his own murderer.

For the body is not given us that we should kill its natural life or work, but only that we kill its wantonness; unless its wantonness were so strong and great that we could not sufficiently resist it without ruin and harm to the natural life. For, as has been said, in the practice of fasting, watching and labor, we are not to look upon the works in themselves, not on the days, not on the number, not on the food, but only on the wanton and lustful Adam, that through them he may be cured of his evil appetite.

21. From this we can judge how wisely or foolishly some women act when they are with child, and how the sick are to be treated. For the foolish women cling so firmly to their fasting that they run the risk of great danger to the fruit of their womb and to themselves, rather than not to fast when the others fast. They make a matter of conscience where there is none, and where there is matter of conscience they make none. This is all the fault of the preachers, because they continually prate of fasting, and never point out its true use, limit, fruit, cause and purpose. So also the sick should be allowed to eat and to drink every day whatever they wish. In brief, where the wantonness of the flesh ceases, there every reason for fasting, watching, laboring, eating

this or that, has already ceased, and there no longer is any binding commandment at all.

But then care must be taken, lest out of this freedom there grow a lazy indifference about killing the wantonness of the flesh; for the roguish Adam is exceedingly tricky in looking for permission for himself, and in pleading the ruin of the body or of the mind; so some men jump right in and say it is neither necessary nor commanded to fast or to mortify the flesh, and are ready to eat this and that without fear, just as if they had for a long time had much experience of fasting, although they have never tried it.

No less are we to guard against offending those who, not sufficiently informed, regard it a great sin if we do not fast or eat as they do. These we must kindly instruct, and not haughtily despise, nor eat this or that in despite of them, but we must tell them the reason why it is right to do so, and thus gradually lead them to a correct understanding. But if they are stubborn and will not listen, we must let them alone, and do as we know it is right to do.

22. The second form of discipline which we receive at the hands of others, is when men or devils cause us suffering, as when our property is taken, our body sick, and our honor taken away; and everything that may move us to anger, impatience and unrest. For God's work rules in us according to His wisdom, not according to our wisdom, according to His purity and chastity, not according to the wantonness of our flesh; for God's work is wisdom and purity, our work is foolishness and impurity, and these shall rest: so in like manner it should rule in us according to His peace, not our anger, impatience and lack of peace. For peace too is God's work, impatience is the work of our flesh; this shall rest and be dead, that we thus in every way keep a spiritual holiday, let our works stand idle, and let God work in us.

Therefore in order to kill our works and the Adam in us, God heaps many temptations upon us, which move us to anger, many sufferings, which rouse us to impatience, and last of all death and the world's abuse; whereby He seeks nothing else than that He may drive out anger, impatience and lack of peace, and attain to His work, that is, to peace, in us. Thus says Isaiah 28, "He does the work of another that He may come to His own work." What does this mean? He sends us suffering and trouble that He may teach us to have patience and peace; He bids us die that He may make us live, until a man, thoroughly trained, becomes so peaceful and quiet that he is not disturbed, whether it go well or ill with him, whether he die or live, be honored or dishonored. There God Himself dwells alone, and there are no works of men. This is rightly keeping and hallowing the day of rest; then a man does not guide himself, then he desires nothing for himself, then nothing troubles him; but God Himself leads him, there is naught but godly pleasure, joy and peace with all other works and virtues.

23. These works He considers so great that He commands us not only to keep the day of rest, but also to hallow it or regard it as holy, whereby He declares that there are no more precious things than suffering, dying, and all manner of misfortune. For they are holy and sanctify a man from his works to God's works, just as a church is consecrated from natural works to the worship of God. Therefore a man shall also recognize them as holy things, be glad and thank God when they come upon him. For when they come they make him holy, so that he fulfils this Commandment and is saved, redeemed from all his sinful works. Thus says David: "Precious in the sight of the Lord is the death of His saints."

In order to strengthen us thereto He has not only commanded us to keep such a rest (for nature is very unwilling to die and to suffer, and it is a bitter day of rest for it to cease from its works and be dead); but He has also comforted us in the Scriptures with many words and told us, Psalm 91, "I will be with him in all his trouble, and will deliver him." Likewise Psalm 34 "The Lord is nigh unto all them that suffer, and will help them."

As if this were not enough, He has given us a powerful, strong example of it, His only, dear Son, Jesus Christ, our Lord, who on the Sabbath lay in the tomb the entire day of rest, free from all His works, and was the first to fulfill this Commandment, although He needed it not for Himself, but only for our comfort, that we also in all suffering and death should be quiet and have peace. Since, as Christ was raised up after His rest and henceforth lives only in God and God in Him, so also shall we by the death of our Adam, which is perfectly accomplished only through natural death and burial, be lifted up into God, that God may live and work in us forever. Lo! these are the three parts of man: reason, desire, aversion; in which all his works are done. These, therefore, must be slain by these three exercises, God's governance, our self-mortification, the hurt done to us by others; and so they must spiritually rest before God, and give Him room for His works.

24. But such works are to be done and such sufferings to be endured in faith and in sure confidence of God's favor, in order that, as has been said, all works remain in the First Commandment and in faith, and that faith, for the sake of which all other commandments and works are ordained, exercise and strengthen itself in them. See, therefore, what a pretty, golden ring these three Commandments and their works naturally form, and how from the First Commandment and faith the Second flows on to the Third, and the Third in turn drives through the Second up into the First. For the first work is to believe, to have a good heart and confidence toward God. From this flows the second good work, to praise God's Name, to confess His grace, to give all honor to Him alone. Then follows the third, to worship by praying, hearing God's Word, thinking of and considering God's benefits, and in addition chastising one's self, and keeping the body under.

But when the evil spirit perceives such faith, such honoring of God and such worship, he rages and stirs up persecution, attacks body, goods, honor and life, brings upon us sickness, poverty, shame and death, which God so permits and ordains. See, here begins the second work, or the second rest of the Third Commandment; by this faith is very greatly tried, even as gold in the fire. For it is a great thing to retain a sure confidence in God, although He sends us death, shame, sickness, poverty; and in this cruel form of wrath to regard Him as our all-gracious Father, as must be done in this work of the Third Commandment. Here suffering contains faith, that it must call upon God's Name and praise it in such suffering, and so it comes through the Third Commandment into the Second again; and through that very calling on the Name of God and praise, faith grows, and becomes conscious of itself, and so strengthens itself, through the two works of the Third and of the Second Commandment. Thus faith goes out into the works and through the works comes to itself again; just as the sun goes forth unto its setting and comes again unto its rising. For this reason the Scriptures associate the day with peaceful living in works, the night with passive living in adversity, and faith lives and works, goes out and comes in, in both, as Christ says, John chapter 9.

25. This order of good works we pray in the Lord's Prayer. The first is this, that we say: "Our Father, Who art in heaven"; these are the words of the first work of faith, which, according to the First Commandment, does not doubt that it has a gracious Father in heaven. The second: "Hallowed be Thy Name," in which faith asks that God's Name, praise and honor be glorified, and calls upon it in every need, as the Second Commandment says. The third: "Thy kingdom come," in which we pray for the true Sabbath and rest, peaceful cessation of our works, that God's work alone be done in us, and so God rule in us as in His own kingdom, as He says, Luke xvii, "Behold, God's kingdom is nowhere else except within you." The fourth petition is "Thy will be done"; in which we pray that we may keep and have the Seven Commandments of the Second Table, in which faith is exercised toward our neighbor; just as in the first three it is exercised in works toward God alone. And these are the petitions in which stands the word "Thou, Thy, Thy, Thy," because they seek

only what belongs to God; all the others say "our, us, our," etc; for in them we pray for our goods and blessedness.

Let this, then, suffice as a plain, hasty explanation of the First Table of Moses, pointing out to simple folk what are the highest of good works.

The Second Table follows.

Thou Shalt Honor Thy Father and Thy Mother: The Fourth (Fifth) Commandment

1. From this Commandment we learn that after the excellent works of the first three Commandments there are no better works than to obey and serve all those who are set over us as superiors. For this reason also disobedience is a greater sin than murder, unchastity, theft and dishonesty, and all that these may include. For we can in no better way learn how to distinguish between greater and lesser sins than by noting the order of the Commandments of God, although there are distinctions also within the works of each Commandment. For who does not know that to curse is a greater sin than to be angry, to strike than to curse, to strike father and mother more than to strike anyone else? Thus these seven Commandments teach us how we are to exercise ourselves in good works toward men, and first of all toward our superiors.

The first work is that we honor our own father and mother. And this honor consists not only in respectful demeanor, but in this: that we obey them, look up to, esteem and heed their words and example, accept what they say, keep silent and endure their treatment of us, so long as it is not contrary to the first three Commandments; in addition, when they need it, that we provide them with food, clothing and shelter. For not for nothing has He said: "Thou shalt honor them"; He does not say: "Thou shalt love them," although this also must be done. But honor is higher than mere love and includes a certain fear, which unites with love, and causes a man to fear offending them more than he fears the punishment. Just as there is fear in the honor we pay a sanctuary, and yet we do not flee from it as from a punishment, but draw near to it all the more. Such a fear mingled with love is the true honor; the other fear without any love is that which we have toward things which we despise or flee from, as we fear the hangman or punishment. There is no honor in that, for it is a fear without all love, nay, fear that has with it hatred and enmity. Of this we have a proverb of St. Jerome: What we fear, that we also hate. With such a fear God does not wish to be feared or honored, nor to have us honor our parents; but with the first, which is mingled with love and confidence.

2. This work appears easy, but few regard it aright. For where the parents are truly pious and love their children not according to the flesh, but (as they ought) instruct and direct them by words and works to serve God according to the first three Commandments, there the child's own will is constantly broken, and it must do, leave undone, and suffer what its nature would most gladly do otherwise; and thereby it finds occasion to despise its parents, to murmur against them, or to do worse things. There love and fear depart, unless they have God's grace. In like manner, when they punish and chastise, as they ought (at times even unjustly, which, however, does not harm the soul's salvation), our evil nature resents the correction. Beside all this, there are some so wicked that they are ashamed of their parents because of poverty, lowly birth, deformity or dishonor, and allow these things to influence them more than the high Commandment of God, Who is above all things, and has with benevolent intent given them such parents, to exercise and try them in His Commandment. But the matter becomes still worse when the child has children of its own; then love descends to them, and detracts very much from the love and honor toward the parents.

But what is said and commanded of parents must also be understood of those who, when the parents are dead or absent, take their place, such as relatives, god-parents, sponsors, temporal lords and spiritual fathers. For every one must be ruled and be subject to other men. Wherefore we here see again how many good works are taught in this Commandment, since in it all our life is made subject to other men.

Hence it comes that obedience is so highly praised and all virtue and good works are included in it.

3. There is another dishonoring of parents, much more dangerous and subtle than this first, which adorns itself and passes for a real honor; that is, when a child has its own way, and the parents through natural love allow it. Here there is indeed mutual honor, here there is mutual love, and on all sides it is a precious thing, parents and child take mutual pleasure in one another.

This plague is so common that instances of the first form of dishonoring are very seldom seen. This is due to the fact that the parents are blinded, and neither know nor honor God according to the first three Commandments; hence also they cannot see what the children lack, and how they ought to teach and train them. For this reason they train them for worldly honors, pleasure and possessions, that they may by all means please men and reach high positions: this the children like, and they obey very gladly without gainsaying.

Thus God's Commandment secretly comes to naught while all seems good, and that is fulfilled which is written in the Prophets Isaiah and Jeremiah, that the children are destroyed by their own parents, and they do like the king Manasseh, who sacrificed his own son to the idol Moloch and burned him, 2 Kings 21 What else is it but to sacrifice one's own child to the idol and to burn it, when parents train their children more in the way of the world than in the way of God? let them go their way, and be burned up in worldly pleasure, love, enjoyment, possessions and honor, but let God's love and honor and the desire of eternal blessings be quenched in them?

O how perilous it is to be a father or a mother, where flesh and blood are supreme! For, truly, the knowledge and fulfillment of the first three and the last six Commandments depends altogether upon this Commandment; since parents are commanded to teach them to their children, as Psalm 78 says, "How strictly has He commanded our fathers, that they should make known God's Commandments to their children, that the generation to come might know them and declare them to their children's children." This also is the reason why God bids us honor our parents, that is, to love them with fear; for that other love is without fear, therefore it is more dishonor than honor.

Now see whether everyone does not have good works enough to do, whether he be father or child. But we blind men leave this untouched, and seek all sorts of other works which are not commanded.

4. Now where parents are foolish and train their children after the fashion of the world, the children are in no way to obey them; for God, according to the first three Commandments, is to be more highly regarded than the parents. But training after the fashion of the world I call it, when they teach them to seek no more than pleasure, honor and possessions of this world or its power.

To wear decent clothes and to seek an honest living is a necessity, and not sin. Yet the heart of a child must be taught to be sorry that this miserable earthly life cannot well be lived, or even begun, without the striving after more adornment and more possessions than are necessary for the protection of the body against cold and for nourishment. Thus the child must be taught to grieve that, without its own will, it must do the world's will and play the fool with the rest of men, and endure such evil for the sake of something better and to avoid something worse. So Queen Esther wore her royal crown, and yet said to God, "Thou knowest, that the sign of my high estate, which is upon my head, has never yet delighted me, and I abhor it as a menstruous rag, and never wear it when I am by myself, but when I must do it and go before the people." The heart that is so minded wears adornment without peril; for it wears and does not wear, dances and does not dance, lives well and does not live well. And these are the secret souls, hidden brides of Christ, but they are rare; for it is hard not to delight in great adornment and parade. Thus St. Cecilia wore golden clothes at the command of her parents, but within against her body she wore a garment of hair.

Here some men say: "How then could I bring my children into society, and marry them honorably? I must make some display." Tell me, are not these the words of a heart which despairs of God, and trusts more on its own providing than on God's care? Whereas St. Peter teaches and says, I. Peter 5, "Cast all your care upon Him, and be certain that He cares for you." It is a sign that they have never yet thanked God for their children, have never yet rightly prayed for them, have never yet commended them to Him; otherwise they would know and have experienced that they ought to ask God also for the marriage dower of their children, and await it from Him. Therefore also He permits them to go their way, with cares and worries, and yet succeed poorly.

5. Thus it is true, as men say, that parents, although they had nothing else to do, could attain salvation by training their own children; if they rightly train them to God's service, they will indeed have both hands full of good works to do. For what else are here the hungry, thirsty, naked, imprisoned, sick, strangers, than the souls of your own children? with whom God makes of your house a hospital, and sets you over them as chief nurse, to wait on them, to give them good words and works as meat and drink, that they may learn to trust, believe and fear God, and to place their hope on Him, to honor His Name, not to swear nor curse, to mortify themselves by praying, fasting, watching, working, to attend worship and to hear God's Word, and to keep the Sabbath, that they may learn to despise temporal things, to bear misfortune calmly, and not to fear death nor to love this life.

See, what great lessons are these, how many good works you have before you in your home, with your child, that needs all these things like a hungry, thirsty, naked, poor, imprisoned, sick soul. O what a blessed marriage and home were that where such parents were to be found! Truly it would be a real Church, a chosen cloister, yea, a paradise. Of such says Psalm 128:1: "Blessed are they that fear God, and walk in His Commandments; thou shalt eat of the labor of thine hands; therefore thou shalt be happy, and it shall be well with thee. Thy wife shall be as a fruitful vine in thine house, and thy children shall be as the young scions of laden olive trees about thy table. Behold, thus shall the man be blessed, that feareth the Lord," etc. Where are such parents? Where are they that ask after good works? Here none wishes to come. Why? God has commanded it; the devil, flesh and blood pull away from it; it makes no show, therefore it counts for nothing. Here this husband runs to St. James, that wife vows a pilgrimage to Our Lady; no one vows that he will properly govern and teach himself and his child to the honor of God; he leaves behind those whom God has commanded him to keep in body and soul, and would serve God in some other place, which has not been commanded him. Such perversity no bishop forbids, no preacher corrects; nay, for covetousness' sake they confirm it and daily only invent more pilgrimages, elevations of saints, indulgence-fairs. God have pity on such blindness.

6. On the other hand, parents cannot earn eternal punishment in any way more easily than by neglecting their own children in their own home, and not teaching them the things which have been spoken of above. Of what help is it, that they kill themselves with fasting, praying, making pilgrimages, and do all manner of good works? God will, after all, not ask them about these things at their death and in the day of judgment, but will require of them the children whom He entrusted to them. This is shown by that word of Christ, Luke 23, "Ye daughters of Jerusalem, weep not for me, but for yourselves and for your children. The days are coming, in which they shall say: Blessed are the wombs that never bare, and the paps which never gave suck." Why shall they lament, except because all their condemnation comes from their own children? If they had not had children, perhaps they might have been saved. Truly, these words ought to open the eyes of parents, that they may have regard to the souls of their children, so

that the poor children be not deceived by their false, fleshly love, as if they had rightly honored their parents when they are not angry with them, or are obedient in worldly matters, by which their self-will is strengthened; although the Commandment places the parents in honor for the very purpose that the self-will of the children may be broken, and that the children may become humble and meek.

Just as it has been said of the other Commandments, that they are to be fulfilled in the chief work, so here too let no one suppose that the training and teaching of his children is sufficient of itself, except it be done in confidence of divine favor, so that a man doubt not that he is well pleasing to God in his works, and that he let such works be nothing else than an exhortation and exercise of his faith, that he trust God and look to Him for blessings and a gracious will; without which faith no work lives, or is good and acceptable; for many heathen have trained their children beautifully, but it is all lost, because of their unbelief.

7. The second work of this Commandment is to honor and obey the spiritual mother, the holy Christian Church, the spiritual power, so that we conform to what she commands, forbids, appoints, orders, binds and looses, and honor, fear and love the spiritual authority as we honor, love and fear our natural parents, and yield to it in all things which are not contrary to the first three Commandments.

Now with regard to this work, things are almost worse than with regard to the first. The spiritual authority should punish sin with the ban and with laws, and constrain its spiritual children to be good, in order that they might have reason to do this work and to exercise themselves in obeying and honoring it. Such zeal one does not see now; they act toward their subjects like the mothers who forsake their children and run after their lovers, as Hosea chapter 2 says; they do not preach, they do not teach, they do not hinder, they do not punish, and there is no spiritual government at all left in Christendom.

What can I say of this work? A few fast-days and feast-days are left, and these had better be done away with. But no one gives this a thought, and there is nothing left except the ban for debt, and this should not be. But spiritual authority should look to it, that adultery, unchastity, usury, gluttony, worldly show, excessive adornment, and such like open sin and shame might be most severely punished and corrected; and they should properly manage the endowments, monastic houses, parishes and schools, and earnestly maintain worship in them, provide for the young people, boys and girls, in schools and cloisters, with learned, pious men as teachers, that they might all be well trained, and so the older people give a good example and Christendom be filled and adorned with fine young people. So St. Paul teaches his disciple Titus, that he should rightly instruct and govern all classes, young and old, men and women. But now he goes to school who wishes; he is taught who governs and teaches himself; nay, it has, alas! come to such a pass that the places where good should be taught have become schools of knavery, and no one at all takes thought for the wild youth.

8. If the above order prevailed, one could say how honor and obedience should be given to the spiritual authority. But now the case is like that of the natural parents who let their children do as they please; at present the spiritual authority threatens, dispenses, takes money, and pardons more than it has power to pardon. I will here refrain from saying more; we see more of it than is good; greed holds the reins, and just what should be forbidden is taught; and it is clearly seen that the spiritual estate is in all things more worldly than the worldly estate itself. Meanwhile Christendom must be ruined, and this Commandment perish.

If there were a bishop who would zealously provide for all these classes, supervise, make visitations and be faithful as he ought, truly, one city would be too much for him. For in the time of the Apostles, when Christendom was at its best estate, each city had a bishop, although the smallest part of the inhabitants were Christians. How may things go when one bishop wants to have so much, another so much, this one the whole world, that one the fourth of it.

It is time that we pray God for mercy. Of spiritual power we have much; but of spiritual government nothing or little. Meanwhile may he help who can, that endowments, monastic houses, parishes and schools be well established and managed; and it would also be one of the works of the spiritual authority that it lessen the number of endowments, monastic houses and schools, where they cannot be cared for. It is much better that there be no monastic house or endowment than that there be evil government in them, whereby God is the more provoked to anger.

9. Since, then, the authorities so entirely neglect their work, and are perverted, it must assuredly follow that they misuse their power, and undertake other and evil works, just as parents do when they give some command contrary to God. Here we must be wise; for the Apostle has said, that those times shall be perilous in which such authorities shall rule. For it seems as if we resisted their power if we do not do and leave undone all that they prescribe. Therefore we must take hold of the first three Commandments and the First Table, and be certain that no man, neither bishop, nor pope, nor angel, may command or determine anything that is contrary to or hinders these three Commandments, or does not help them; and if they attempt such things, it is not valid and amounts to nothing; and we also sin if we follow and obey, or even tolerate such acts.

From this it is easy to understand that the commands of fasting do not include the sick, the pregnant women, or those who for other reasons cannot fast without injury. And, to rise higher, in our time nothing comes from Rome but a fair of spiritual wares, which are openly and shamelessly bought and sold, indulgences, parishes, monastic houses, bishoprics, provostships, benefices, and everything that has ever been founded to God's service far and wide; whereby not only is all money and wealth of the world drawn and driven to Rome (for this would be the smallest harm), but the parishes, bishoprics and prelacies are torn to pieces, deserted, laid waste, and so the people are neglected, God's Word and God's Name and honor come to naught, and faith is destroyed, so that at last such institutions and offices fall into the hands not only of unlearned and unfit men, but the greater part into the hands of the Romans, the greatest villains in the world. Thus what has been founded for God's service, for the instruction, government and improvement of the people, must now serve the stable-boys, mule-drivers, yea, not to use plainer language, Roman whores and knaves; yet we have no more thanks than that they mock us for it as fools.

10. If then such unbearable abuses are all carried on in the Name of God and St. Peter, just as if God's Name and the spiritual power were instituted to blaspheme God's honor, to destroy Christendom, body and soul: we are indeed in duty bound to resist in a proper way as much as we can. And here we must do like pious children whose parents have become insane, and first see by what right that which has been founded for God's service in our lands, or has been ordained to provide for our children, must be allowed to do its work in Rome, and to lapse here, where it ought to serve. How can we be so foolish?

Since then bishops and spiritual prelates stand idle in this matter, offer no opposition or are afraid, and thus allow Christendom to perish, it is our duty first of all humbly to call upon God for help to prevent this thing, then to put our hand to work to the same end, send the courtesans and those who bear letters from Rome about their business, in a reasonable, gentle way inform them that, if they wish to care for their parishes properly, they shall live in them and improve the people by preaching or by good example; or if not, and they do live in Rome or elsewhere, lay waste and debauch the churches, then let the pope feed them, whom they serve. It is not fitting that we support the pope's servants, his people, yes, his knaves and whores, to the destruction and injury of our souls.

Lo! these are the true Turks, whom the kings, princes and the nobility ought to attack first: not seeking thereby their own benefit, but only the improvement of Christendom, and the prevention of the blasphemy and disgracing of the divine Name; and so to deal with the clergy as with a father who has lost his sense and wits; who, if one did not restrain him and resist him (although with all humility and honor), might destroy child, heir and everybody. Thus we are to honor Roman authority as our highest father; and yet, since they have gone mad and lost their senses, not allow them to do what they attempt, lest Christendom be destroyed thereby.

11. Some think, this should be referred to a General Council. To this I say: No! For we have had many councils in which this has been proposed, namely, at Constance, Basel and the last Roman Council; but nothing has been accomplished, and things have grown ever worse, Moreover, such councils are entirely useless, since Roman wisdom has contrived the device that the kings and princes must beforehand take an oath to let the Romans remain what they are and keep what they have, and so has put up a bar to ward off all reformation, to retain protection and liberty for all their knavery, although this oath is demanded, forced and taken contrary to God and the law, and by it the doors are locked against the Holy Spirit, Who should rule the councils. But this would be the best, and also the only remedy remaining, if kings, princes, nobility, cities and communities themselves began and opened a way for reformation, so that the bishops and clergy, who now are afraid, would have reason to follow. For here nothing else shall and must be considered except God's first three Commandments, against which neither Rome, nor heaven nor earth can command or forbid anything. And the ban or threatening with which they think they can prevent this, amounts

to nothing; just as it amounts to nothing if an insane father severely threatens the son who restrains him or locks him up.

12. The third work of this Commandment is to obey the temporal authority, as Paul teaches, Romans 13, and Titus 3, and St. Peter, 1 Peter 2: "Submit yourselves to the king as supreme, and to the princes as his ambassadors, and to all the ordinances of the worldly power." But it is the work of the temporal power to protect its subjects, and to punish thievery, robbery, and adultery, as St. Paul says in Romans 13: "It beareth not the sword in vain; it serves God with it, to the terror of evil doers, and to the protection of the good."

Here men sin in two ways. First, if they lie to the government, deceive it, and are disloyal, neither obey nor do as it has ordered and commanded, whether with their bodies or their possessions. For even if the government does injustice, as the King of Babylon did to the people of Israel, yet God would have it obeyed, without treachery and deception. Secondly, when men speak evil of the government and curse it, and when a man cannot revenge himself and abuses the government with grumbling and evil words, publicly or secretly.

In all this we are to regard that which St. Peter bids us regard, namely, that its power, whether it do right or wrong, cannot harm the soul, but only the body and property; unless indeed it should try openly to compel us to do wrong against God or men; as in former days when the magistrates were not yet Christians, and as the Turk is now said to do. For to suffer wrong destroys no one's soul, nay, it improves the soul, although it inflicts loss upon the body and property; but to do wrong, that destroys the soul, although it should gain all the world's wealth.

13. This also is the reason why there is not such great danger in the temporal power as in the spiritual, when it does wrong. For the

temporal power can do no harm, I since it has nothing to do with preaching and faith and the first three Commandments. But the spiritual power does harm not only when it does wrong, but also when it neglects its duty and busies itself with other things, even if they were better than the very best works of the temporal power. Therefore, we must resist it when it does not do right, and not resist the temporal power although it does wrong. For the poor people believe and do as they see the spiritual power believing and doing; if they are not set an example and are not taught, then they also believe nothing and do nothing; since this power is instituted for no other reason than to lead the people in faith to God. All this is not found in the temporal power; for it may do and leave undone what it will, my faith to God still goes its way and works its works, because I need not believe what it believes.

Therefore, also, the temporal power is a very small thing in God's sight, and far too slightly regarded by Him, that for its sake, whether it do right or wrong, we should resist, become disobedient and quarrel. On the other hand, the spiritual power is an exceeding great blessing, and far too precious in His eyes, that the very least of Christians should endure and keep silent, if it departs a hair's breadth from its own duty, not to say when it does the very opposite of its duty, as we now see it do every day.

14. In this power also there is much abuse. First, when it follows the flatterers, which is a common and especially harmful plague of this power, against which no one can sufficiently guard and protect himself. Here it is led by the nose, and oppresses the common people, becomes a government of the like of which a heathen says: "The spider-webs catch the small flies, but the mill-stones roll through." So the laws, ordinances and government of one and the same authority hold the small men, and the great are free; and where the prince is not himself so wise that he needs nobody's advice, or has such a standing

that they fear him, there will and must be (unless God should do a special wonder) a childish government.

For this reason God has considered evil, unfit rulers the greatest of plagues, as He threatens, Isaiah 3, "I will take away from them every man of valor, and will give children to be their princes and babes to rule over them." Four plagues God has named in Scripture, Ezekiel 14. The first and slightest, which also David chose, is pestilence, the second is famine, the third is war, the fourth is all manner of evil beasts, such as lions, wolves, serpents, dragons; these are the wicked rulers. For where these are, the land is destroyed, not only in body and property, as in the others, but also in honor, discipline, virtue and the soul's salvation. For pestilence and famine make people good and rich; but war and wicked rulers bring to naught everything that has to do with temporal and eternal possessions.

15. A prince must also be very wise and not at all times undertake to enforce his own will, although he may have the authority and the very best cause. For it is a far nobler virtue to endure wrong to one's authority than to risk property and person, if it is advantageous to the subjects; since worldly rights attach only to temporal goods.

Hence, it is a very foolish saying: I have a right to it, therefore I will take it by storm and keep it, although all sorts of misfortune may come to others thereby. So we read of the Emperor Octavianus, that he did not wish to make war, however just his cause might be, unless there were sure indications of greater benefit than harm, or at least that the harm would not be intolerable, and said: "War is like fishing with a golden net; the loss risked is always greater than the catch can be." For he who guides a wagon must walk far otherwise than if he were walking alone; when alone he may walk, jump, and do as he will; but when he drives, he must so guide and adapt himself that the wagon and horses can follow him, and regard that more than his own will. So also a prince leads a multitude with him and must not walk and act as he wills, but as the multitude can, considering their need and advantage more than his will and pleasure. For when a prince rules after his own mad will and follows his own opinion, he is like a mad driver, who rushes straight ahead with horse and wagon, through bushes, thorns, ditches, water, uphill and down dale, regardless of roads and bridges; he will not drive long, all will go to smash.

Therefore it would be most profitable for rulers, that they read, or have read to them, from youth on, the histories, both in sacred and in secular books, in which they would find more examples and skill in ruling than in all the books of law; as we read that the kings of Persia did, Esther 6. For examples and histories benefit and teach more than the laws and statutes: there actual experience teaches, here untried and uncertain words.

16. Three special, distinct works all rulers might do in our times, particularly in our lands.

First, to make an end of the horrible gluttony and drunkenness, not only because of the excess, but also because of its expense. For through seasonings and spices and the like, without which men could well live, no little loss of temporal wealth has come and daily is coming upon our lands. To prevent these two great evils would truly give the temporal power enough to do, for the inroads they have made are wide and deep. And how could those in power serve God better and thereby also improve their own land?

Secondly, to forbid the excessive cost of clothing, whereby so much wealth is wasted, and yet only the world and the flesh are served; it is fearful to think that such abuse is to be found among the people who have been pledged, baptized and consecrated to Christ, the Crucified, and who should bear the Cross after Him and prepare for the life to come by dying daily. If some men erred through ignorance, it might be borne; but that it is practiced so freely, without punishment, without shame, without hindrance, nay, that praise and fame are sought thereby, this is indeed an unchristian thing.

Thirdly, to drive out the usurious buying of rent-charges, which in the whole world ruins, consumes and troubles all lands, peoples and cities through its cunning form, by which it appears not to be usury, while in truth it is worse than usury, because men are not on their guard against it as against open usury. See, these are the three Jews, as men say, who suck the whole world dry. Here princes ought not to sleep, nor be lazy, if they would give a good account of their office to God.

17. Here too ought to be mentioned the knavery which is practiced by officials and other episcopal and spiritual officers, who ban, load, hunt and drive the poor people with great burdens, as long as a penny remains. This ought to be prevented by the temporal sword, since there is no other help or remedy.

O, would God in heaven, that some time a government might be established that would do away with the public bawdy-houses, as was done among the people of Israel! It is indeed an unchristian sight, that public houses of sin are maintained among Christians, a thing formerly altogether unheard of. It should be a rule that boys and girls should be married early and such vice be prevented. Such a rule and custom ought to be sought for by both the spiritual and the temporal power. If it was possible among the Jews, why should it not also be possible among Christians? Nay, if it is possible in villages, towns and some cities, as we all see, why should it not be possible everywhere?

But the trouble is, there is no real government in the world. No one wants to work, therefore the mechanics must give their workmen holiday: then they are free and no one can tame them. But if there were a rule that they must do as they are bid, and no one would give them work in other places, this evil would to a large extent be mended. God help us! I fear that here the wish is far greater than the hope; but this does not excuse us.

Now see, here only a few works of magistrates are indicated, but they are so good and so many, that they have superabundant good works to do every hour and could constantly serve God. But these works, like the others, should also be done in faith, yea, be an exercise of faith, so that no one expect to please God by the works, but by confident trust in His favor do such works only to the honor and praise of his gracious God, thereby to serve and benefit his neighbor.

18. The fourth work of this Commandment is obedience of servants and workmen toward their lords and ladies, masters and mistresses. Of this St. Paul says, Titus ii: "Thou shalt exhort servants that they highly honor their masters, be obedient, do what pleases them, not cheating them nor opposing them"; for this reason also: because they thereby bring the doctrine of Christ and our faith into good repute, that the heathen cannot complain of us and be offended. St. Peter also says: "Servants, be subject to your masters, for the fear of God, not only to the good and gentle, but also to the froward and harsh. For this is acceptable with God, if a man suffers harshness, being innocent."

Now there is the greatest complaint in the world about servants and working men, that they are disobedient, unfaithful, unmannerly, and over-reaching; this is a plague sent of God. And truly, this is the one work of servants whereby they may be saved; truly they need not make pilgrimages or do this thing or the other; they have enough to do if their heart is only set on this, that they gladly do and leave undone what they know pleases their masters and mistresses, and all this in a simple faith; not that they would by their works gain much merit, but that they do it all in the confidence of divine favor (in which all merits are to be found), purely for nothing, out of the love and good-will toward God which grows out of such confidence. And all such works they should think of as an exercise and exhortation ever to strengthen their faith and confidence more and more. For, as has now been frequently said, this faith makes all works good, yea, it must do them and be the master-workman.

19. On the other hand, the masters and mistresses should not rule their servants, maids and workingmen roughly, not look to all things too closely, occasionally overlook something, and for peace' sake make allowances. For it is not possible that everything be done perfectly at all times among any class of men, as long as we live on earth in imperfection. Of this St. Paul says, Colossians 4, "Masters, do unto your servants that which is just and equal, knowing that ye also have a Master in heaven." Therefore as the masters do not wish God to deal too sharply with them, but that many things be overlooked through grace, they also should be so much the more gentle toward their servants, and overlook some things, and yet have a care that the servants do right and learn to fear God.

But see now, what good works a householder and a mistress can do, how finely God offers us all good works so near at hand, so manifold, so continuously, that we have no need of asking after good works, and might well forget the other showy, far-off, invented works of men, such as making pilgrimages, building churches, seeking indulgence, and the like.

Here I ought naturally also to say how a wife ought to be obedient, subject to her husband as to her superior, give way to him, keep silent and give up to him, where it is a matter not contrary to God's commands. On the other hand, the husband should love his wife, overlook a little, and not deal strictly with her, of which matter St. Peter and St. Paul have said much. But this has its place in the further explanation of the Ten Commandments, and is easily inferred from these passages.

20. But all that has been said of these works is included in these two, obedience and considerateness. Obedience is the duty of subjects, considerateness that of masters, that they take care to rule their subjects well, deal kindly with them, and do everything whereby they may

benefit and help them. That is their way to heaven, and these are the best works they can do on earth; with these they are more acceptable to God than if without these they did nothing but miracles. So says St. Paul, Romans 12: "He that ruleth, let him do it with diligence"; as who should say: "Let him not allow himself to be led astray by what other people or classes of people do; let him not look to this work or to that, whether it be splendid or obscure; but let him look to his own position, and think only how he may benefit those who are subject to him; by this let him stand, nor let himself be torn from it, although heaven stood open before him, nor be driven from it, although hell were chasing him. This is the right road that leads him to heaven."

Oh, if a man were so to regard himself and his position, and attended to its duties alone, how rich in good works would he be in a short time, so quietly and secretly that no one would notice it except God alone! But now we let all this go, and one runs to the Carthusians, another to this place, a third to that, just as if good works and God's Commandments had been thrown into corners and hidden; although it is written in Proverbs 1, that divine wisdom crieth out her commandments publicly in the streets, in the midst of the people and in the gates of the cities; which means that they are present in profusion in all places, in all stations of life and at all times, and we do not see them, but in our blindness look for them elsewhere. This Christ declared, Matthew 24: "If they shall say unto you: Lo, here is Christ, or there, believe it not. If they shall say: Behold, He is in the desert, go not forth; behold, He is in the secret chambers, believe it not; they are false prophets and false Christs."

21. Again, obedience is the duty of subjects, that they direct all their diligence and effort to do and to leave undone what their over-lords desire of them, that they do not allow themselves to be torn or driven from this, whatever another do. Let no man think that he lives well or does good works, whether it be prayer or fasting, or by whatever

name it may be called, if he does not earnestly and diligently exercise himself in this.

But if it should happen, as it often does, that the temporal power and authorities, as they are called, should urge a subject to do contrary to the Commandments of God, or hinder him from doing them, there obedience ends, and that duty is annulled. Here a man must say as St. Peter says to the rulers of the Jews: "We ought to obey God rather than men." He did not say: "We must not obey men"; for that would be wrong; but he said: "God rather than men." Thus, if a prince desired to go to war, and his cause was manifestly unrighteous, we should not follow nor help him at all; since God has commanded that we shall not kill our neighbor, nor do him injustice. Likewise, if he bade us bear false witness, steal, lie or deceive and the like. Here we ought rather give up goods, honor, body, and life, that God's Commandments may stand.

The four preceding Commandments have their works in the understanding, that is, they take a man captive, rule him and make him subject, so that he rule not himself, approve not himself, think not highly of himself; but in humility know himself and allow himself to be led, that pride be prevented. The following Commandments deal with the passions and lust of men, that these also be killed.

Thou Shalt Not Kill: The Fifth (Sixth) Commandment

1. The passions of anger and revenge, of which the Fifth Commandment says, "Thou shalt not kill." This Commandment has one work, which however includes many and dispels many vices, and is called meekness. Now this is of two kinds. The one has a beautiful splendor, and there is nothing back of it. This we practice toward our friends and those who do us good and give us pleasure with goods, honor and favor, or who do not offend us with words nor with deeds. Such meekness irrational animals have, lions and snakes, Jews, Turks, knaves, murderers, bad women. These are all content and gentle when men do what they want, or let them alone; and yet there are not a few who, deceived by such worthless meekness, cover over their anger and excuse it, saying: "I would indeed not be angry, if I were left alone." Certainly, my good man, so the evil spirit also would be meek if he had his own way. Dissatisfaction and resentment overwhelm you in order that they may show you how full of anger and wickedness you are, that you may be admonished to strive after meekness and to drive out anger.

The second form of meekness is good through and through, that which is shown toward opponents and enemies, does them no harm, does not revenge itself, does not curse nor revile, does not speak evil of them, does not meditate evil against them, although they had taken away goods, honor, life, friends and everything. Nay, where it is possible, it returns good for evil, speaks well of them, thinks well of them, prays for them. Of this Christ says, Matthew v: "Do good to them that despitefully use you. Pray for them that persecute you and revile you." And Paul, Romans 12: "Bless them which curse you, and by no means curse them, but do good to them."

2. Behold how this precious, excellent work has been lost among Christians, so that nothing now everywhere prevails except strife, war, quarreling, anger, hatred, envy, back-biting, cursing, slandering, injuring, vengeance, and all manner of angry works and words; and yet, with all this, we have our many holidays, hear masses, say our prayers, establish churches, and more such spiritual finery, which God has not commanded. We shine resplendently and excessively, as if we were the most holy Christians there ever were. And so because of these mirrors and masks we allow God's Commandment to go to complete ruin, and no one considers or examines himself, how near or how far he be from meekness and the fulfillment of this Commandment; although God has said, that not he who does such works, but he who keeps His Commandments, shall enter into eternal life.

Now, since no one lives on earth upon whom God does not bestow an enemy and opponent as a proof of his own anger and wickedness, that is, one who afflicts him in goods, honor, body or friends, and thereby tries whether anger is still present, whether he can be well-disposed toward his enemy, speak well of him, do good to him, and not intend any evil against him; let him come forward who asks what he shall do that he may do good works, please God and be saved. Let him set his enemy before him, keep him constantly before the eyes of his heart, as an exercise whereby he may curb his spirit and train his heart to think kindly of his enemy, wish him well, care for him and pray for him; and then, when opportunity offers, speak well of him and do good to him. Let him who will, try this and if he find not enough to do all his life long, he may convict me of lying, and say that my contention was wrong. But if this is what God desires, and if He will be paid in no other coin, of what avail is it, that we busy ourselves with other great works which are not commanded, and neglect this? Therefore God says, Matthew 5, "I say unto you, that whosoever is angry with his neighbor, is in danger of the judgment; but whosoever shall say to his brother, Thou fool (that is, all manner of invective, cursing, reviling, slandering), he shall be in danger of everlasting fire." What remains then for the outward act, striking, wounding, killing, injuring, etc., if the thoughts and words of anger are so severely condemned?

3. But where there is true meekness, there the heart is pained at every evil which happens to one's enemy. And these are the true children and heirs of God and brethren of Christ, Whose heart was so pained for us all when He died on the holy Cross. Even so we see a pious judge passing sentence upon the criminal with sorrow, and regretting the death which the law imposes. Here the act seems to be one of anger and harshness. So thoroughly good is meekness that even in such works of anger it remains, nay, it torments the heart most sorely when it must be angry and severe.

But here we must watch, that we be not meek contrary to God's honor and Commandment. For it is written of Moses that he was the very meekest man on earth, and yet, when the Jews had worshiped the golden calf and provoked God to anger, he put many of them to death, and thereby made atonement before God. Likewise it is not fitting that the magistrates should be idle and allow sin to have sway, and that we say nothing. My own possessions, my honor, my injury, I must not regard, nor grow angry because of them; but God's honor and Commandment we must protect, and injury or injustice to our neighbor we must prevent, the magistrates with the sword, the rest of us with reproof and rebuke, yet always with pity for those who have merited the punishment.

This high, noble, sweet work can easily be learned, if we perform it in faith, and as an exercise of faith. For if faith does not doubt the favor of God nor question that God is gracious, it will become quite easy for a man to be gracious and favorable to his neighbor, however much he may have sinned; for we have sinned much more against God. Behold, a short Commandment this, but it presents a long, mighty exercise of good works and of faith.

Thou Shalt Not Commit Adultery: The Sixth (Seventh) Commandment

1. In this Commandment too a good work is commanded, which includes much and drives away much vice; it is called purity, or chastity, of which much is written and preached, and it is well known to everyone, only that it is not as carefully observed and practiced as other works which are not commanded. So ready are we to do what is not commanded and to leave undone what is commanded. We see that the world is full of shameful works of unchastity, indecent words, tales and ditties, temptation to which is daily increased through gluttony and drunkenness, idleness and frippery. Yet we go our way as if we were Christians; when we have been to church, have said our little prayer, have observed the fasts and feasts, then we think our whole duty is done.

Now, if no other work were commanded but chastity alone, we would all have enough to do with this one; so perilous and raging a vice is unchastity. It rages in all our members: in the thoughts of our hearts, in the seeing of our eyes, in the hearing of our ears, in the words of our mouth, in the works of our hands and feet and all our body. To control all these requires labor and effort; and thus the Commandments of God teach us how great truly good works are, nay, that it is impossible for us of our own strength to conceive a good work, to say nothing of attempting or doing it. St. Augustine says, that among all the conflicts of the Christian the conflict of chastity is the hardest, for the one reason alone, that it continues daily without ceasing, and chastity seldom prevails. This all the saints have wept over and lamented, as St. Paul does, Romans 7: "I find in me, that is in my flesh, no good thing." '

2. If this work of chastity is to be permanent, it will drive to many other good works, to fasting and temperance over against gluttony and drunkenness, to watching and early rising over against laziness and excessive sleep, to work and labor over against idleness. For gluttony, drunkenness, lying late abed, loafing and being without work are weapons of unchastity, with which chastity is quickly overcome. On the other hand, the holy Apostle Paul calls fasting, watching and labor godly weapons, with which unchastity is mastered; but, as has been said above, these exercises must do no more than overcome unchastity, and not pervert nature.

Above all this, the strongest defense is prayer and the Word of God; namely, that when evil lust stirs, a man flee to prayer, call upon God's mercy and help, read and meditate on the Gospel, and in it consider Christ's sufferings. Thus says Psalm 137:9: "Happy shall he be, that taketh and dasheth the little ones of Babylon against the rock," that is, if the heart runs to the Lord Christ with its evil thoughts while they are yet young and just beginning; for Christ is a Rock, on which they are ground to powder and come to naught.

See, here each one will find enough to do with himself, and more than enough, and will be given many good works to do within himself. But now no one uses prayer, fasting, watching, labor for this purpose, but men stop in these works as if they were in themselves the whole purpose, although they should be arranged so as to fulfill the work of this Commandment and purify us daily more and more.

Some have also indicated more things which should be avoided, such as soft beds and clothes, that we should avoid excessive adornment, and neither associate nor talk with members of the opposite sex, nor even look upon them, and whatsoever else may be conducive to chastity. In all these things no one can fix a definite rule and measure. Each one must watch himself and see what things are needful to him for chastity, in what quantity and how long they help him to be chaste, that he may thus choose and observe them for himself; if he cannot do this, let him for a time give himself up to be controlled by another, who may hold him to such observance until he can learn to rule himself. This was the purpose for which the monastic houses were established of old, to teach young people discipline and purity.

3. In this work a good strong faith is a great help, more noticeably so than in almost any other; so that for this reason also Isaiah 11 says that "faith is a girdle of the reins," that is, a guard of chastity. For he who so lives that he looks to God for all grace, takes pleasure in spiritual purity; therefore he can so much more easily resist fleshly impurity: and in such faith the Spirit tells him of a certainty how he shall avoid evil thoughts and everything that is repugnant to chastity. For as the faith in divine favor lives without ceasing and works in all works, so it also does not cease its admonitions in all things that are pleasing to God or displease Him; as St. John says in his Epistle: "Ye need not that any man teach you: for the divine anointing, that is, the Spirit of God, teacheth you of all things."

Yet we must not despair if we are not soon rid of the temptation, nor by any means imagine that we are free from it as long as we live, and we must regard it only as an incentive and admonition to prayer, fasting, watching, laboring, and to other exercises for the quenching of the flesh, especially to the practice and exercise of faith in God. For that chastity is not precious which is at ease, but that which is at war with unchastity, and fights, and without ceasing drives out all the poison with which the flesh and the evil spirit attack it. Thus St. Peter says, "I beseech you, abstain from fleshly desires and lusts, which war always against the soul." And St. Paul, Romans 6, "Ye shall not obey the body in its lusts." In these and like passages it is shown that no one is without evil lust; but that everyone shall and must daily fight against it. But although this brings uneasiness and pain, it is none the less a work that gives pleasure, in which we shall have our comfort and satisfaction. For they who think they make an end of temptation by yielding to it, only set themselves on fire the more; and although for a time it is quiet, it comes again with more strength another time, and finds the nature weaker than before.

Thou Shalt Not Steal: The Seventh (Eighth) Commandment

1. This Commandment also has a work, which embraces very many good works, and is opposed to many vices, and is called in German Mildigkeit, "benevolence;" which is a work ready to help and serve every one with one's goods. And it fights not only against theft and robbery, but against all stinting in temporal goods which men may practice toward one another: such as greed, usury, overcharging and plating wares that sell as solid, counterfeit wares, short measures and weights, and who could tell all the ready, novel, clever tricks, which multiply daily in every trade, by which every one seeks his own gain through the other's loss, and forgets the rule which says: "What ye wish that others do to you, that do ye also to them." If everyone kept this rule before his eyes in his trade, business, and dealings with his neighbor, he would readily find how he ought to buy and sell, take and give, lend and give for nothing, promise and keep his promise, and the like. And when we consider the world in its doings, how greed controls all business, we would not only find enough to do, if we would make an honorable living before God, but also be overcome with dread and fear for this perilous, miserable life, which is so exceedingly overburdened, entangled and taken captive with cares of this temporal life and dishonest seeking of gain.

2. Therefore the Wise Man says not in vain: "Happy is the rich man, who is found without blemish, who does not run after gold, and has not set his confidence in the treasures of money. Who is he? We will praise him, that he has done wondrous things in his life." As if he would say: "None such is found, or very few indeed." Yea, they are very few who notice and recognize such lust for gold in themselves. For greed has here a very beautiful, fine cover for its shame, which is called provision

for the body and natural need, under cover of which it accumulates wealth beyond all limits and is never satisfied; so that he who would in this matter keep himself clean, must truly, as he says, do miracles or wondrous things in his life.

Now see, if a man wish not only to do good works, but even miracles, which God may praise and be pleased with, what need has he to look elsewhere? Let him take heed to himself, and see to it that he run not after gold, nor set his trust on money, but let the gold run after him, and money wait on his favor, and let him love none of these things nor set his heart on them; then he is the true, generous, wonderworking, happy man, as Job 31 says: "I have never yet: relied upon gold, and never yet made gold my hope and confidence." And Psalm 62: "If riches increase, set not your heart upon them." So Christ also teaches, Matthew 6, that we shall take no thought, what we shall eat and drink and wherewithal we shall be clothed, since God cares for this, and knows that we have need of all these things.

But some say: "Yes, rely upon that, take no thought, and see whether a roasted chicken will fly into your mouth!" I do not say that a man shall not labor and seek a living; but he shall not worry, not be greedy, not despair, thinking that he will not have enough; for in Adam we are all condemned to labor, when God says to him, Genesis 3, "In the sweat of thy face shalt thou eat bread." And Job 5, "As the birds to flying, so is man born unto labor." Now the birds fly without worry and greed, and so we also should labor without worry and greed; but if you do worry and are greedy, wishing that the roasted chicken fly into your mouth: worry and be greedy, and see whether you will thereby fulfill God's Commandment and be saved!

3. This work faith teaches of itself. For if the heart looks for divine favor and relies upon it, how is it possible that a man should be greedy and worry? He must be sure beyond a doubt that God cares for him; therefore he does not cling to money; he uses it also with cheerful liberality for the benefit of his neighbor, and knows well that

he will have enough, however much he may give away. For his God, Whom he trusts, will not lie to him nor forsake him, as it is written in Psalm 37:25 "I have been young, and now am old; never have I seen a believing man, who trusts God, that is a righteous man, forsaken, or his child begging bread." Therefore the Apostle calls no other sin idolatry except covetousness, because this sin shows most plainly that it does not trust God for anything, expects more good from its money than from God; and, as has been said, it is by such confidence that God is truly honored or dishonored.

And, indeed, in this Commandment it can be clearly seen how all good works must be done in faith; for here every one most surely feels that the cause of covetousness is distrust and the cause of liberality is faith. For because a man trusts God, he is generous and does not doubt that he will always have enough; on the other hand, a man is covetous and worries because he does not trust God. Now, as in this Commandment faith is the master-workman and the doer of the good work of liberality, so it is also in all the other Commandments, and without such faith liberality is of no worth, but rather a careless squandering of money.

4. By this we are also to know that this liberality shall extend even to enemies and opponents. For what manner of good deed is that, if we are liberal only to our friends? As Christ teaches, Luke vi, even a wicked man does that to another who is his friend. Besides, the brute beasts also do good and are generous to their kind. Therefore a Christian must rise higher, let his liberality serve also the undeserving, evil-doers, enemies, and the ungrateful, even as his heavenly Father makes His sun to rise on good and evil, and the rain to fall on the grateful and ungrateful.

But here it will be found how hard it is to do good works according to God's Commandment, how nature squirms, twists and writhes in its opposition to it, although it does the good works of its own choice easily and gladly. Therefore take your enemies, the ungrateful, and do good to them; then you will find how near you are to this Commandment or how far from it, and how all your life you will always have to do with the practice of this work. For if your enemy needs you and you do not help him when you can, it is just the same as if you had stolen what belonged to him, for you owed it to him to help him. So says St. Ambrose, "Feed the hungry; if you do not feed him, you have, as far as you are concerned, slain him." And in this Commandment are included the works of mercy, which Christ will require at men's hands at the last day.

But the magistrates and cities ought to see to it that the vagabonds, pilgrims and mendicants from foreign lands be debarred, or at least allowed only under restrictions and rules, so that knaves be not permitted to run at large under the guise of mendicants, and their knavery, of which there now is much, be prohibited. I have spoken at greater length of this Commandment in the Treatise on Usury.

Thou Shalt Not Bear False Witness Against Thy Neighbor: The Eighth Ninth) Commandment

1. This Commandment seems small, and yet is so great, that he who would rightly keep it must risk and imperil life and limb, goods and honor, friends and all that he has; and yet it includes no more than the work of that small member, the tongue, and is called in German Wahrheit sagen, "telling the truth" and, where there is need, gainsaying lies; so that it forbids many evil works of the tongue. First: those which are committed by speaking, and those which are committed by keeping silent. By speaking, when a man has an unjust law-suit, and wants to prove and maintain his case by a false argument, catch his neighbor with subtlety, produce everything that strengthens and furthers his own cause, and withhold and discount everything that furthers his neighbor's good cause; in doing which he does not do to his neighbor as he would have his neighbor do to him. This some men do for the sake of gain, some to avoid loss or shame, thereby seeking their own advantage more than God's Commandment, and excuse themselves by saying: *Vigilanti jura subveniunt*, "the law helps him who watches"; just as if it were not as much their duty to watch for their neighbor's cause as for their own. Thus they intentionally allow their neighbor's cause to be lost, although they know that it is just. This evil is at present so common that I fear no court is held and no suit tried but that one side sins against this Commandment. And even when they cannot accomplish it, they yet have the unrighteous spirit and will, so that they would wish the neighbor's just cause to be lost and their unjust cause to prosper. This sin is most frequent when the opponent is a prominent man or an enemy. For a man wants to revenge himself on his enemy: but the ill will of a man of prominence he does not wish to bring upon himself; and then begins the flattering and fawning, or, on the other hand, the withholding of the truth.

Here no one is willing to run the risk of disfavor and displeasure, loss and danger for the truth's sake; and so God's Commandment must perish. And this is almost universally the way of the world. He who would keep this Commandment, would have both hands full doing only those good works which concern the tongue. And then, how many are there who allow themselves to be silenced and swerved aside from the truth by presents and gifts! so that in all places it is truly a high, great, rare work, not to be a false witness against one's neighbor.

2. There is a second bearing of witness to the truth, which is still greater, with which we must fight against the evil spirits; and this concerns not temporal matters, but the Gospel and the truth of faith, which the evil spirit has at no time been able to endure, and always so manages that the great among men, whom it is hard to resist, must oppose and persecute it. Of which it is written in Psalm 82, "Rid the poor out of the hand of the wicked, and help the forsaken to maintain his just cause."

Such persecution, it is true, has now become infrequent; but that is the fault of the spiritual prelates, who do not stir up the Gospel, but let it perish, and so have abandoned the very thing because of which such witnessing and persecution should arise; and in its place they teach us their own law and what pleases them. For this reason the devil also does not stir, since by vanquishing the Gospel he has also vanquished faith in Christ, and everything goes as he wishes. But if the Gospel should be stirred up and be heard again, without doubt the whole world would be aroused and moved, and the greater portion of the kings, princes, bishops, doctors and clergy, and all that is great, would oppose it and rage against it, as has always happened when the Word of God has come to light; for the world cannot endure what comes from God. This is proved in Christ, Who was and is the very greatest and most precious and best of all that God has; yet the world not only did not receive Him, but persecuted Him more cruelly than all others who had ever come forth from God.

151

Therefore, as at that time, so at all times there are few who stand by the divine truth, and imperil and risk life and limb, goods and honor, and all that they have, as Christ has foretold: "Ye shall be hated of all men for My Name's sake." And: "Many of them shall be offended in Me." Yea, if this truth were attacked by peasants, herdsmen, stable-boys and men of no standing, who would not be willing and able to confess it and to bear witness to it? But when the pope, and the bishops, together with princes and kings attack it, all men flee, keep silent, dissemble, in order that they may not lose goods, honor, favor and life.

3. Why do they do this? Because they have no faith in God, and expect nothing good from Him. For where such faith and confidence are, there is also a bold, defiant, fearless heart, that ventures and stands by the truth, though it cost life or cloak, though it be against pope or kings; as we see that the martyrs did. For such a heart is satisfied and rests easy because it has a gracious, loving God. Therefore it despises all the favor, grace, goods and honor of men, lets them come and go as they please; as is written in Psalm 15: "He contemneth them that contemn God, and honoreth them that fear the Lord"; that is, the tyrants, the mighty, who persecute the truth and despise God, he does not fear, he does not regard them, he despiseth them; on the other hand, those who are persecuted for the truth's sake, and fear God more than men, to these he clings, these he defends, these he honors, let it vex whom it may; as it is written of Moses, Hebrews xi, that he stood by his brethren, regardless of the mighty king of Egypt.

Lo, in this Commandment again you see briefly that faith must be the master-workman in this work also, so that without it no one has courage to do this work: so entirely are all works comprised in faith, as has now been often said. Therefore, apart from faith all works are dead, however good the form and name they bear. For as no one does the work of this Commandment except he be firm and fearless in the confidence of divine favor; so also he does no work of any other Commandment without the same faith: thus every one may easily by this Commandment test and weigh himself whether he be a Christian and truly believe in Christ, and thus whether he is doing good works or no. Now we see how the Almighty God has not only set our Lord Jesus Christ before us that we should believe in Him with such confidence, but also holds before us in Him an example of this same confidence and of such good works, to the end that we should believe in Him, follow Him and abide in Him forever; as He says, John xiv: "I am the Way, the Truth and the Life,"--the Way, in which we follow Him; the Truth, that we believe in Him; the Life, that we live in Him forever.

From all this it is now manifest that all other works, which are not commanded, are perilous and easily known: such as building churches, beautifying them, making pilgrimages, and all that is written at so great length in the Canon Law and has misled and burdened the world and ruined it, made uneasy consciences, silenced and weakened faith, and has not said how a man, although he neglect all else, has enough to do with all his powers to keep the Commandments of God, and can never do all the good works which he is commanded to do; why then does he seek others, which are neither necessary nor commanded, and neglect those that are necessary and commanded?

Thou Shalt Not Covet: The Ninth and Tenth Commandments (The Tenth Commandment)

The last two Commandments, which forbid evil desires of the body for pleasure and for temporal goods, are clear in themselves; these evil desires do no harm to our neighbor, and yet they continue unto the grave, and the strife in us against them endures unto death; therefore these two Commandments are drawn together by St. Paul into one, Romans chapter 7, and are set as a goal unto which we do not attain, and only in our thoughts reach after until death. For no one has ever been so holy that he felt in himself no evil inclination, especially when occasion and temptation were offered. For original sin is born in us by nature, and may be checked, but not entirely uprooted, except through the death of the body; which for this reason is profitable and a thing to be desired. To this may God help us. Amen.

APPENDIX 1: Martin Luther's 95 Theses

DISPUTATION OF DOCTOR MARTIN LUTHER

ON THE POWER AND EFFICACY OF INDULGENCES

OCTOBER 31, 1517

Out of love for the truth and the desire to bring it to light, the following propositions will be discussed at Wittenberg, under the presidency of the Reverend Father Martin Luther, Master of Arts and of Sacred Theology, and Lecturer in Ordinary on the same at that place. Wherefore he requests that those who are unable to be present and debate orally with us, may do so by letter. In the Name our Lord Jesus Christ. Amen.

1. Our Lord and Master Jesus Christ, when He said "*Poenitentiam agite*", willed that the whole life of believers should be repentance.

2. This word cannot be understood to mean sacramental penance, i.e., confession and satisfaction, which is administered by the priests.

3. Yet it means not inward repentance only; nay, there is no inward repentance which does not outwardly work divers mortifications of the flesh.

4. The penalty of sin, therefore, continues so long as hatred of self continues; for this is the true inward repentance, and continues until our entrance into the kingdom of heaven.

Martin Luther

5. The pope does not intend to remit, and cannot remit any penalties other than those which he has imposed either by his own authority or by that of the Canons.

6. The pope cannot remit any guilt, except by declaring that it has been remitted by God and by assenting to God's remission; though, to be sure, he may grant remission in cases reserved to his judgment. If his right to grant remission in such cases were despised, the guilt would remain entirely unforgiven.

7. God remits guilt to no one whom He does not, at the same time, humble in all things and bring into subjection to His vicar, the priest.

8. The penitential canons are imposed only on the living, and, according to them, nothing should be imposed on the dying.

9. Therefore the Holy Spirit in the pope is kind to us, because in his decrees he always makes exception of the article of death and of necessity.

10. Ignorant and wicked are the doings of those priests who, in the case of the dying, reserve canonical penances for purgatory.

11. This changing of the canonical penalty to the penalty of purgatory is quite evidently one of the tares that were sown while the bishops slept.

12. In former times the canonical penalties were imposed not after, but before absolution, as tests of true contrition.

13. The dying are freed by death from all penalties; they are already dead to canonical rules, and have a right to be released from them.

14. The imperfect health [of soul], that is to say, the imperfect love, of the dying brings with it, of necessity, great fear; and the smaller the love, the greater is the fear.

15. This fear and horror is sufficient of itself alone (to say nothing of other things) to constitute the penalty of purgatory, since it is very near to the horror of despair.

16. Hell, purgatory, and heaven seem to differ as do despair, almost-despair, and the assurance of safety.

17. With souls in purgatory it seems necessary that horror should grow less and love increase.

18. It seems unproved, either by reason or Scripture, that they are outside the state of merit, that is to say, of increasing love.

19. Again, it seems unproved that they, or at least that all of them, are certain or assured of their own blessedness, though we may be quite certain of it.

20. Therefore by "full remission of all penalties" the pope means not actually "of all," but only of those imposed by himself.

21. Therefore those preachers of indulgences are in error, who say that by the pope's indulgences a man is freed from every penalty, and saved;

22. Whereas he remits to souls in purgatory no penalty which, according to the canons, they would have had to pay in this life.

23. If it is at all possible to grant to any one the remission of all penalties whatsoever, it is certain that this remission can be granted only to the most perfect, that is, to the very fewest.

24. It must needs be, therefore, that the greater part of the people are deceived by that indiscriminate and high-sounding promise of release from penalty.

25. The power which the pope has, in a general way, over purgatory, is just like the power which any bishop or curate has, in a special way, within his own diocese or parish.

26. The pope does well when he grants remission to souls in purgatory, not by the power of the keys (which he does not possess), but by way of intercession.

27. They preach man who say that so soon as the penny jingles into the money-box, the soul flies out (of purgatory).

28. It is certain that when the penny jingles into the money-box, gain and avarice can be increased, but the result of the intercession of the Church is in the power of God alone.

29. Who knows whether all the souls in purgatory wish to be bought out of it, as in the legend of Sts. Severinus and Paschal.

30. No one is sure that his own contrition is sincere; much less that he has attained full remission.

31. Rare as is the man that is truly penitent, so rare is also the man who truly buys indulgences, i.e., such men are most rare.

32. They will be condemned eternally, together with their teachers, who believe themselves sure of their salvation because they have letters of pardon.

33. Men must be on their guard against those who say that the pope's pardons are that inestimable gift of God by which man is reconciled to Him;

34. For these "graces of pardon" concern only the penalties of sacramental satisfaction, and these are appointed by man.

35. They preach no Christian doctrine who teach that contrition is not necessary in those who intend to buy souls out of purgatory or to buy confessionalia.

36. Every truly repentant Christian has a right to full remission of penalty and guilt, even without letters of pardon.

37. Every true Christian, whether living or dead, has part in all the blessings of Christ and the Church; and this is granted him by God, even without letters of pardon.

38. Nevertheless, the remission and participation in the blessings of the Church which are granted by the pope are in no way to be despised, for they are, as I have said, the declaration of divine remission.

39. It is most difficult, even for the very keenest theologians, at one and the same time to commend to the people the abundance of pardons and the need of true contrition.

40. True contrition seeks and loves penalties, but liberal pardons only relax penalties and cause them to be hated, or at least, furnish an occasion for hating them.

41. Apostolic pardons are to be preached with caution, lest the people may falsely think them preferable to other good works of love.

42. Christians are to be taught that the pope does not intend the buying of pardons to be compared in any way to works of mercy.

43. Christians are to be taught that he who gives to the poor or lends to the needy does a better work than buying pardons;

44. Because love grows by works of love, and man becomes better; but by pardons man does not grow better, only more free from penalty.

45. Christians are to be taught that he who sees a man in need, and passes him by, and gives [his money] for pardons, purchases not the indulgences of the pope, but the indignation of God.

46. Christians are to be taught that unless they have more than they need, they are bound to keep back what is necessary for their own families, and by no means to squander it on pardons.

47. Christians are to be taught that the buying of pardons is a matter of free will, and not of commandment.

48. Christians are to be taught that the pope, in granting pardons, needs, and therefore desires, their devout prayer for him more than the money they bring.

49. Christians are to be taught that the pope's pardons are useful, if they do not put their trust in them; but altogether harmful, if through them they lose their fear of God.

50. Christians are to be taught that if the pope knew the exactions of the pardon-preachers, he would rather that St. Peter's church should go to ashes, than that it should be built up with the skin, flesh and bones of his sheep.

51. Christians are to be taught that it would be the pope's wish, as it is his duty, to give of his own money to very many of those from whom certain hawkers of pardons cajole money, even though the church of St. Peter might have to be sold.

52. The assurance of salvation by letters of pardon is vain, even though the commissary, nay, even though the pope himself, were to stake his soul upon it.

53. They are enemies of Christ and of the pope, who bid the Word of God be altogether silent in some Churches, in order that pardons may be preached in others.

54. Injury is done the Word of God when, in the same sermon, an equal or a longer time is spent on pardons than on this Word.

55. It must be the intention of the pope that if pardons, which are a very small thing, are celebrated with one bell, with single processions and ceremonies, then the Gospel, which is the very greatest thing, should be preached with a hundred bells, a hundred processions, a hundred ceremonies.

56. The "treasures of the Church," out of which the pope grants indulgences, are not sufficiently named or known among the people of Christ.

57. That they are not temporal treasures is certainly evident, for many of the vendors do not pour out such treasures so easily, but only gather them.

58. Nor are they the merits of Christ and the Saints, for even without the pope, these always work grace for the inner man, and the cross, death, and hell for the outward man.

59. St. Lawrence said that the treasures of the Church were the Church's poor, but he spoke according to the usage of the word in his own time.

60. Without rashness we say that the keys of the Church, given by Christ's merit, are that treasure;

61. For it is clear that for the remission of penalties and of reserved cases, the power of the pope is of itself sufficient.

62. The true treasure of the Church is the Most Holy Gospel of the glory and the grace of God.

63. But this treasure is naturally most odious, for it makes the first to be last.

64. On the other hand, the treasure of indulgences is naturally most acceptable, for it makes the last to be first.

65. Therefore the treasures of the Gospel are nets with which they formerly were wont to fish for men of riches.

66. The treasures of the indulgences are nets with which they now fish for the riches of men.

67. The indulgences which the preachers cry as the "greatest graces" are known to be truly such, in so far as they promote gain.

68. Yet they are in truth the very smallest graces compared with the grace of God and the piety of the Cross.

69. Bishops and curates are bound to admit the commissaries of apostolic pardons, with all reverence.

70. But still more are they bound to strain all their eyes and attend with all their ears, lest these men preach their own dreams instead of the commission of the pope.

71. He who speaks against the truth of apostolic pardons, let him be anathema and accursed!

72. But he who guards against the lust and license of the pardon-preachers, let him be blessed!

73. The pope justly thunders against those who, by any art, contrive the injury of the traffic in pardons.

74. But much more does he intend to thunder against those who use the pretext of pardons to contrive the injury of holy love and truth.

75. To think the papal pardons so great that they could absolve a man even if he had committed an impossible sin and violated the Mother of God--this is madness.

76. We say, on the contrary, that the papal pardons are not able to remove the very least of venial sins, so far as its guilt is concerned.

77. It is said that even St. Peter, if he were now Pope, could not bestow greater graces; this is blasphemy against St. Peter and against the pope.

78. We say, on the contrary, that even the present pope, and any pope at all, has greater graces at his disposal; to wit, the Gospel, powers, gifts of healing, etc., as it is written in I. Corinthians xii.

79. To say that the cross, emblazoned with the papal arms, which is set up [by the preachers of indulgences], is of equal worth with the Cross of Christ, is blasphemy.

80. The bishops, curates and theologians who allow such talk to be spread among the people, will have an account to render.

81. This unbridled preaching of pardons makes it no easy matter, even for learned men, to rescue the reverence due to the pope from slander, or even from the shrewd questionings of the laity.

82. To wit: "Why does not the pope empty purgatory, for the sake of holy love and of the dire need of the souls that are there, if he redeems an infinite number of souls for the sake of miserable money with which to build a Church? The former reasons would be most just; the latter is most trivial."

83. Again: "Why are mortuary and anniversary masses for the dead continued, and why does he not return or permit the withdrawal of the endowments founded on their behalf, since it is wrong to pray for the redeemed?"

84. Again: "What is this new piety of God and the pope, that for money they allow a man who is impious and their enemy to buy out of purgatory the pious soul of a friend of God, and do not rather, because of that pious and beloved soul's own need, free it for pure love's sake?"

85. Again: "Why are the penitential canons long since in actual fact and through disuse abrogated and dead, now satisfied by the granting of indulgences, as though they were still alive and in force?"

86. Again:--"Why does not the pope, whose wealth is today greater than the riches of the richest, build just this one church of St. Peter with his own money, rather than with the money of poor believers?"

87. Again:--"What is it that the pope remits, and what participation does he grant to those who, by perfect contrition, have a right to full remission and participation?"

88. Again:--"What greater blessing could come to the Church than if the pope were to do a hundred times a day what he now does once, and bestow on every believer these remissions and participations?"

89. "Since the pope, by his pardons, seeks the salvation of souls rather than money, why does he suspend the indulgences and pardons granted heretofore, since these have equal efficacy?"

90. To repress these arguments and scruples of the laity by force alone, and not to resolve them by giving reasons, is to expose the Church and the pope to the ridicule of their enemies, and to make Christians unhappy.

91. If, therefore, pardons were preached according to the spirit and mind of the pope, all these doubts would be readily resolved; nay, they would not exist.

92. Away, then, with all those prophets who say to the people of Christ, "Peace, peace," and there is no peace!

93. Blessed be all those prophets who say to the people of Christ, "Cross, cross," and there is no cross!

94. Christians are to be exhorted that they be diligent in following Christ, their Head, through penalties, deaths, and hell;

95. And thus be confident of entering into heaven rather through many tribulations, than through the assurance of peace.

APPENDIX 2: Luther's Address
Before the Diet of Worms

MOST SERENE EMPEROR, AND YOU ILLUSTRIOUS
PRINCES AND GRACIOUS LORDS:

I this day appear before you in all humility, according to your
command, and I implore your majesty and your august highnesses,
by the mercies of God, to listen with favor to the defense of a cause
which I am well assured is just and right. I ask pardon, if by reason
of my ignorance, I am wanting in the manners that befit a court; for
I have not been brought up in king's palaces, but in the seclusion of
a cloister.

Two questions were yesterday put to me by his imperial majesty;
the first, whether I was the author of the books whose titles were read;
the second, whether I wished to revoke or defend the doctrine I have
taught. I answered the first, and I adhere to that answer.

As to the second, I have composed writings on very different subjects.
In some I have discussed Faith and Good Works, in a spirit at once
so pure, clear, and Christian, that even my adversaries themselves,
far from finding anything to censure, confess that these writings are
profitable, and deserve to be perused by devout persons. The pope's
bull, violent as it is, acknowledges this. What, then, should I be doing
if I were now to retract these writings? Wretched man! I alone, of all
men living, should be abandoning truths approved by the unanimous
voice of friends and enemies, and opposing doctrines that the whole
world glories in confessing!

I have composed, secondly, certain works against popery, wherein I
have attacked such as by false doctrines, irregular lives, and scandalous
examples, afflict the Christian world, and ruin the bodies and souls

of men. And is not this confirmed by the grief of all who fear God? Is it not manifest that the laws and human doctrines of the popes entangle, vex, and distress the consciences of the faithful, while the crying and endless extortions of Rome engulf the property and wealth of Christendom, and more particularly of this illustrious nation?

If I were to revoke what I have written on that subject, what should I do…. but strengthen this tyranny, and open a wider door to so many and flagrant impieties? Bearing down all resistance with fresh fury, we should behold these proud men swell, foam, and rage more than ever! And not merely would the yoke which now weighs down Christians be made more grinding by my retractation—it would thereby become, so to speak, lawful,—for, by my retractation, it would receive confirmation from your most serene majesty, and all the States of the Empire. Great God! I should thus be like to an infamous cloak, used to hid and cover over every kind of malice and tyranny.

In the third and last place, I have written some books against private individuals, who had undertaken to defend the tyranny of Rome by destroying the faith. I freely confess that I may have attacked such persons with more violence than was consistent with my profession as an ecclesiastic: I do not think of myself as a saint; but neither can I retract these books. because I should, by so doing, sanction the impieties of my opponents, and they would thence take occasion to crush God's people with still more cruelty.

Yet, as I am a mere man, and not God, I will defend myself after the example of Jesus Christ, who said: "If I have spoken evil, bear witness against me" (John 18:23). How much more should I, who am but dust and ashes, and so prone to error, desire that everyone should bring forward what he can against my doctrine.

Therefore, most serene emperor, and you illustrious princes, and all, whether high or low, who hear me, I implore you by the mercies of God to prove to me by the writings of the prophets and apostles that I am in error. As soon as I shall be convinced, I will instantly retract all my errors, and will myself be the first to seize my writings, and commit them to the flames.

What I have just said I think will clearly show that I have well considered and weighed the dangers to which I am exposing myself; but far from being dismayed by them, I rejoice exceedingly to see the Gospel this day, as of old, a cause of disturbance and disagreement. It is the character and destiny of God's word. "I came not to send peace unto the earth, but a sword," said Jesus Christ. God is wonderful and awful in His counsels. Let us have a care, lest in our endeavors to arrest discords, we be bound to fight against the holy word of God and bring down upon our heads a frightful deluge of inextricable dangers, present disaster, and everlasting desolations.... Let us have a care lest the reign of the young and noble prince, the Emperor Charles, on whom, next to God, we build so many hopes, should not only commence, but continue and terminate its course under the most fatal auspices. I might cite examples drawn from the oracles of God. I might speak of Pharaohs, of kings of Babylon, or of Israel, who were never more contributing to their own ruin than when, by measures in appearances most prudent, they thought to establish their authority! "God removeth the mountains and they know not" (Job 9:5).

In speaking thus, I do not suppose that such noble princes have need of my poor judgment; but I wish to acquit myself of a duty that Germany has a right to expect from her children. And so commending myself to your august majesty, and your most serene highnesses, I beseech you in all humility, not to permit the hatred of my enemies to rain upon me an indignation I have not deserved.

Since your most serene majesty and your high mightinesses require of me a simple, clear and direct answer, I will give one, and it is this: I cannot submit my faith either to the pope or to the council, because it is as clear as noonday that they have fallen into error and even into glaring inconsistency with themselves. If, then, I am not convinced by proof from Holy Scripture, or by cogent reasons, if I am not satisfied by the very text I have cited, and if my judgment is not in this way brought into subjection to God's word, I neither can nor will retract anything; for it cannot be right for a Christian to speak against his country. I stand here and can say no more.

God help me. Amen

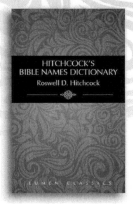

ISBN: 978-0-9835608-9-0

Hitchcock's Bible Names Directory

by Roswell D. Hitchcock

Power Through Prayer

by Edward M. Bounds

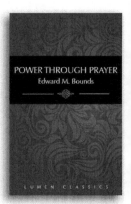

ISBN: 978-0-9835608-5-2

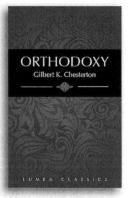

ISBN: 978-0-9835608-6-9

Orthodoxy

by G.K. Chesterton

The Overcoming Life

by Dwight L Moody

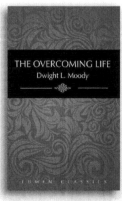

ISBN: 978-1-939900-03-6

...m Lumen Classics

The Pilgrim's Progress

by John Bunyan

ISBN: 978-0-9835608-8-3

In His Steps

by Charles M. Sheldon

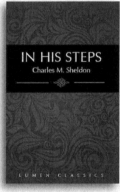

ISBN: 978-0-9835608-7-6

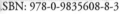

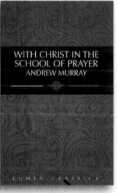

With Christ in the
School of Prayer

by Andrew Murray

ISBN: 978-1-939900-01-2